Teacher Made Materials That Really Teach!

Judy Herr
Yvonne Libby Larson
Dawn Tennyson-Grimm

THOMSON
DELMAR LEARNING

Australia Canada Mexico Singapore Spain United Kingdom United States

THOMSON
™
DELMAR LEARNING

Teacher Made Materials That Really Teach!
Judy Herr, Yvonne Libby Larson, and Dawn Tennyson-Grimm

Vice President, Career Education SBU
Dawn Gerrain

Acquisitions Editor
Erin J. O'Connor

Editorial Assistant
Ivy Ip

Director of Production
Wendy A. Troeger

Production Editor
Joy Kocsis

Technology Project Manager
Joseph Saba

Director of Marketing
Donna J. Lewis

Channel Manager
Nigar Hale

Cover Design
Joseph Villanova

Composition
Stratford Publishing Services, Inc.

For permission to use material from this text or product, contact us by:
Tel: (800) 730-2214
Fax: (800) 730-2215
www.thomsonrights.com

Library of Congress Cataloging-in-Publication Data

Herr, Judy.
  Teacher made materials that really teach / Judy Herr, Yvonne Libby Larson, Dawn Tennyson-Grimm.
    p. c.m.
  ISBN 1-40182-428-5
  1. Early childhood education—Activity programs—Handbooks, manuals, etc. 2. Creative activities and seat work—Handbooks, manuals, etc. 3. Teaching—Aids and devices—Handbooks, manuals, etc. I. Libby Larson, Yvonne. II. Tennyson-Grimm, Dawn. III. Title.

  LB1139.35.A37 H47 2003
  371.33—dc21

                                    2002041260

NOTICE TO THE READER

Publisher does not warrant or guarantee any of the products described herein or perform any independent analysis in connection with any of the product information contained herein. Publisher does not assume, and expressly disclaims, any obligation to obtain and include information other than that provided to it by the manufacturer.

The reader is expressly warned to consider and adopt all safety precautions that might be indicated by the activities herein and to avoid all potential hazards. By following the instructions contained herein, the reader willingly assumes all risks in connection with such instructions.

The Publisher makes no representation or warranties of any kind, including but not limited to the warranties of fitness for particular purpose or merchantability, nor are any such representations implied with respect to the material set forth herein, and the publisher takes no responsibility with respect to such material. The publisher shall not be liable for any special, consequential, or exemplary damages resulting, in whole or part, from the readers' use of, or reliance upon, this material.

Table of Contents

Art

Classroom Environment

Dramatic Play

Games

Language Arts

Math

Music and Fingerplays

Science

Social Studies

Contents by Subject

Large Muscle Activities

Math
Charts

Counting and Numerals

Preface

Teacher Made Materials That Really Teach! contains ideas, instructions, and photographs of the materials teachers have prepared to promote the physical, social, emotional, and cognitive growth of young children. Like those of our previous publications, these educational materials are designed to encourage children to be curious and to take initiative by exploring and interacting with other children and adults. Young children learn when their thoughts and experiences interact with materials, ideas, and people. Such interactions should give young children meaningful developmental learning experiences.

The creative, teacher made materials in this book have been used successfully in children's programs in the Child and Family Study Center at the University of Wisconsin-Stout, as well as in kindergarten programs. These materials were designed primarily for preschool and kindergarten children to explore and manipulate during large blocks of time called "center time." (Other educational programs may call this time "self-selected time," "small group time," or "play time.") Many of these materials support solitary activities or activities in small or large groups.

For additional Teacher Made Materials visit our website at:
http://www.earlychilded.delmar.com

Acknowledgments

Between our conceptualization of this book and its completion, many individuals—through their support, encouragement, and creative ideas—helped us. We offer our sincere thanks to all of them.

First, we thank our parents, who fostered our creativity and love of young children.

We thank our husbands, Jim Herr, Troy Larson, and Ryan Grimm, who understand our commitment to the lives of young children.

We thank our typist, Debbie Hass, who so ably transcribed our writing and ideas. We also thank Andrew Bottolfson, who helped with our photography.

Next, we thank our colleagues in early childhood, with whom we have worked at the University of Wisconsin-Stout.

We thank all students majoring in early childhood education at the University of Wisconsin-Stout; the children enrolled in the Child and Family Study Center; and the kindergarten class in the Ridgeland-Dallas Elementary School, who have enjoyed the materials in this book.

We thank the professionals, nationally and internationally, who use *Creative Resources for the Early Childhood Classroom* and who encouraged us to write additional curriculum-related books.

We also thank our editors, Erin J. O'Connor and her assistant Ivy S. Ip, who helped us throughout the publishing process.

We thank the following reviewers, enlisted by Delmar Learning, who provided valuable suggestions and constructive criticism:

Victoria Folds, EdD
Tutor Time Learning Systems
Boca Raton, FL

Jennifer Johnson, MEd
Vance-Granville Community College
Louisburg, NC

Beverly Hugener, MA
Reid State Technical College
Evergreen, AL

Leanna Manna, MA
Villa Maria College
Buffalo, NY

Finally, we thank Jeffrey, Eva, Madelyn and all the other children in the world, who make our efforts worthwhile.

Introduction

Section Organization

Teacher Made Materials That Really Teach is divided into nine curriculum areas commonly found in early childhood programs: art, classroom environment, dramatic play, games, language arts, math, music and fingerplays, science, and social studies. Many of the materials in the section on classroom environment are decorative as well as educational.

Art

Art allows children to plan and think originally. Art involves the senses and imagination. The creative, teacher made materials in this book are designed to encourage creative expression and to foster experimentation with art media. Through exploring materials, children learn many concepts—color, shape, and size, for example. Through hands-on experimentation, sensitivity to tactile and visual experiences improves. Children take pleasure and learn while manipulating and changing materials. Through constructing and using the Crayon and Marker Bundles, for example, children can experiment with cause-and-effect relationships. The materials in this section, like all the others, are designed to promote eye-hand coordination, provide for self-expression, and develop small muscle skills. Some of the materials—Chunk Crayons, Crayon Identification Match, and Fingerpainting in a Bag—reinforce visual discrimination and color recognition skills. Likewise, the Clown Makeup Chart allows children to experiment with cause-and-effect relationships. Additionally, the Squeeze Bottle Art Chart creates an awareness of changes in substances.

Classroom Environment

The teacher made materials in the classroom environment section communicate to children, parents, and other teachers what is expected of them and what is happening in the classroom. A well-planned environment is inviting and interesting and conveys a message. To help the teacher decorate the room, materials related to birthdays are included: Birthday Cakes, Birthday Packages, and Birthday Train. Daily Schedule Charts have been designed to encourage an awareness of the daily classroom routine. The Number of Children in Center Areas has been included to promote self-regulation through clear limits. A Book Return Box helps children learn how to care for books and to cooperate. The Labels for Classroom Areas or Centers provide a print-rich environment and offer the message that writing and reading are meaningful. Finally, responsibility for belongings is encouraged through a Lost and Found Box.

Dramatic Play

Dramatic play lets children try out new roles, problem solve, and make decisions. While imitating others, children learn to understand fears and fantasies by expressing those fears and fantasies. Furthermore, through this process they are able to clarify concepts. To promote role-playing, this section offers props for Goldilocks and the Three Bears, Nylon Mask Puppets, Pot Holder Puppets, Dramatic Play Signs, Dramatic Play Menu, and a Tablecloth Road Map. Puppets are a powerful medium for encouraging children to dramatize their thoughts and feelings. While using puppets, children lose themselves by becoming the characters. As the children learn to cooperate by sharing these materials, social and language skills may also develop.

Games

The games in this book have been included to foster fine motor, gross motor coordination, and social skills. The Summer Fun Lacing Cards, Wallpaper Puzzles, and Sticker Tracing Mazes are excellent activities for self-directed or self-initiated play. Activities for group games—Farmer in the Dell Game Pieces and Bean Bag Toss—are also included.

Language Arts

Carefully selected language arts materials help develop listening, speaking, and writing skills, as well as an appreciation for the printed word. The Alphabet Letter Cards are designed to promote letter identification. Letters make words, and words are the focus of the Chubby Little Snowman materials, which promote auditory memory skills and association between spoken and printed words. The writing center is an important classroom area, because it promotes letter recognition skills, encourages fine motor coordination skills, fosters hand-eye coordination skills, cultivates visual memory, and promotes an interest in the written word. The Humpty Dumpty Chart and Valentine Words can be hung in this area to add aesthetic appeal to the room and to promote exposure to the printed word. Sand Paper Letter Match can be constructed to promote letter recognition skills. Letter recognition skills can also be stimulated through such materials as Object-Word Puzzles, Alphabet Soup Match, and Clothespin Letters and Words.

Math

The focus of math materials for young children should be exploration, discovery, and understanding. The concepts of classification, measurement, position, volume, and number recognition are all included in a well-structured environment. The Jigsaw Puzzles have been designed to promote problem-solving skills. The Coin Sorting Chart allows children to engage in classification—sorting or grouping objects into categories or classes by some distinguishing characteristic. Counting is another basic math skill that must be included in the curriculum. It is an important problem-solving tool, and several materials have been included to encourage counting and to promote numeral recognition skills. Examples include the Mitten Number Sets, Number Cans, Ice Cream Cone Match, Sticker Number Cards, and the Clock Chart.

Music and Fingerplays

Laughter, creativity, enjoyment, freedom, and movement are all encouraged by music and fingerplays. Music is a universal language expressed through voice and body. Music can teach listening skills, sound differences, and language patterns. Children can also develop an appreciation of their cultural heritages through music. In addition to musical skills, some of the teacher made materials in this section—Finding Colors and Three Brown Mice—also promote color recognition skills. A teaching aid is included for introducing the song "Eensie Weensie Spider." Fingerplays like Two Little Apples and the Cookie Jar have been introduced to encourage auditory memory and vocabulary skills.

Science

Children must actively explore and question to understand their world, and science helps them learn to do that. As children observe, wonder, predict, and question, they learn science concepts and develop general knowledge and language skills. The materials in this section are designed to encourage the development of imagination and curiosity. A Weather Chart is included in this section to foster an understanding of the effects of different weather conditions. To encourage children to develop prediction skills, an Absorption Chart and Sink or Float Chart are included. Recipe charts have been included for children to observe changes in substances. Examples include Banana Bobs, Dog Biscuits, and Pudding. To develop an appreciation for living things, a Worm Farm and a Soda Bottle Terrarium are included. Instructions for making Movement Jars are included. Other creative teacher made materials in this section include a Circle Glider Chart, Hand Washing Chart, Sensory Shakers, and Magic Mirror Pictures.

Social Studies

Young children build socialization skills by observing and interacting with the people around them. To become effective citizens, children must understand the social symbols of our society. The teacher made materials in this section are designed to introduce social study concepts. The Good Deed Box and Good Deed Bucket promote kindness, respect, and responsibility. Symbols and holiday customs are introduced and reinforced through Make a Valentine and Make a Halloween Card. Birthday customs are promoted through the Birthday Chart and Birthday Crowns.

Material Organization

All materials in this book have the same format: Developmental Goals, Related Curriculum Themes, Curriculum Areas, Preparation Tools and Materials, Directions, and Teaching/Learning Strategies.

Developmental Goals

Developmental goals are listed for every piece of teacher made material. These goals address the material's value by describing how the children's growth and development can be promoted. For example, by tracing alphabet stencils, the children may learn to:

- recognize letters of the alphabet
- develop eye-hand coordination skills
- develop visual perception skills
- develop appreciation for the printed word
- practice problem solving

Related Curriculum Themes

Themes are general ideas or concepts to which teacher made materials relate. Possible curriculum themes have been included, but the teacher made materials in this book can be adapted to the classroom curriculum theme. Various concepts can usually be developed with any teacher made material.

Varied themes can be taught with one teacher made material. Sample themes include:

Acting	Books	Community Helpers
Air	Boxes	Containers
Animals	Breads	Cooking
Apples	Brushes	Costumes
Art	Bubbles	Counting
Auto Mechanic	Cars and Trucks	Creativity
Bags	Celebrations	Dance
Ballet	Chickens	Designs
Balls	Christmas	Easter
Bells	Circus	Exercise
Birds	Clothes or Clothing	Fairy Tales
Birthdays	Colors	Fall
Bones	Communication	Farm Animals

Fasteners
Feelings
Food
Friends
Frogs
Fruits
Games
Gardens
Gloves
Hair Stylist
Halloween
Health
Hobbies
Holidays
Horses
Hot or Cold
Insects
Insects and Spiders
Instruments
Laundromat
Leaves
Letters
Library
Light
Make Believe
Masks
Mice
Music
My Body

My Center
Me, I'm Special
Measurement
Movement
Numbers
Nursery Rhymes
Nutrition
Occupations
Ocean
Our Senses
Painting
Paper
Pets
Pictures
Plants
Poetry
Puppets
Puzzles
Rabbits
Recipes
Restaurant
Rhymes
Safety
Sand and Soil
Science
Scissors
Seasons
Seeds
Self-Concept

Senses
Shapes
Shovels and Scoops
Sight
Signs
Sink or Float
Sounds
Sports
Stores
Stories
Storytelling
Summer
Symbols
Tools
Touch
Transportation
Trees
Valentine's Day
Water
Weather
Wheels
Wild Animals
Winter
Words
Writing
Writing Tools
Zoo

Curriculum Areas

Curriculum areas may be called "centers" or "content areas" in some programs. This book contains teacher made materials for the art, language arts, large motor, math, music, science, small motor, and social studies areas.

Preparation Tools and Materials

This section lists all the resources you will need to make each teaching aid. To save time, you might want to gather all these items before preparing the material.

Directions

This section outlines the steps for preparing each material. To save time, follow two practices. First, study the photograph(s) in the book. Then, review the directions.

Teaching/Learning Strategies

The purpose of the teaching/learning strategies section is to suggest ways for introducing and using the materials. Some materials, especially many of the games, have specific strategies. Others can be placed in a classroom area for use during self-initiated or self-directed play. For some activities, suggestions have been given to vary and extend the activities.

Using Materials

To plan a developmentally appropriate early childhood curriculum, you must begin with a basic knowledge of how children grow, develop, and learn. When selecting or

adapting activities, consider the needs and interests of your children. Select or design materials that build on the children's experiences. Typically, you will find that four-, five-, six-, and seven-year-old children appear most enthusiastic about the writing center materials. Most three-year-old children and some four-year-olds lack the pre-requisite skills for writing activities. Typically, children of these ages are more interested in painting and drawing. These skills are needed to give the children practice in the small muscle, visual discrimination, and eye-hand coordination skills that are pre-requisites for writing.

Saving Supplies

It is easier to make teacher made materials when you make it a habit to collect supplies on an ongoing basis. To do this, ask the parents of the children in your class to save materials. Begin by sending a letter home, e-mailing a message, or posting a note on the parents' bulletin board. Be specific. State which materials would be most beneficial. Possible supplies to save include:

Paper	Boxes	Fabric
Calendar pictures	Catalogs	Stationery
Gift wrapping paper	Wallpaper books	Stickers
Buttons	Envelopes	Book covers
Pencils	Greeting cards	Rubber stamps
Folders	Newspapers	Berry baskets
Egg cartons	Styrofoam trays	Cube boxes
Tongue depressors	Stationery boxes	Felt pieces
Photographs	Magazines	

Your community can also be a valuable source of recyclable, free, or inexpensive materials. For example, such materials can be solicited from printing companies, grocery stores, junk yards, second-hand stores, pharmacies, fabric and craft stores, decorating stores, carpeting stores, office supply stores, restaurants, photography studios, hair stylist shops, bakeries, flower shops, gift shops, and card shops.

To help you collect recyclable materials, share the following list with your colleagues, parents, and classroom volunteers:

Aluminum foil	Corrugated paper	Plastic bags
Appliance boxes	Drapes	Plastic berry boxes
Beads	Egg cartons	Plastic detergent bottles
Braiding	Felt	Plastic deodorant bottles
Buckles	Flannel	Plastic packing pieces
Buckram	Gloves	Plastic trays
Burlap	Greeting cards	Ribbon
Buttons	Hardboard	Rope
Calendars	Hatboxes	Sandpaper
Canvas	Jewelry	Shoeboxes
Cardboard sheets	Keys	Spools
Cardboard tubes	Magazines	Spray bottles
Carpeting	Measuring cups	Squeeze bottles
Cellophane	Measuring spoons	Stamps
Ceramic tile	Newspapers	Stationery boxes
Coffee cans	Pantyhose containers	Thread
Colored pictures	Paper bags	Tongue depressors
Computer paper	Photographs	Wallpaper
Confetti	Picture frames	Wrapping paper

Using Writing Tools

Children enjoy using various writing tools. You may find that you can create interest by introducing new tools periodically. Consider the following:

Chalk
Colored pens
Crayons
Felt-tip markers: fine, medium, and broad widths
Grease pencils
Oil pastels
Pencils: colored, lead

With supervision, your children can write on a laminated piece of material with permanent broad-tip markers. (Interestingly, these markings can be removed by applying hair spray and wiping immediately.)

In a given classroom, children's developmental abilities usually vary widely. With markers, you can tailor the material to make it developmentally appropriate. For example, a game board could be constructed of tagboard and laminated. Then, the lettering could be printed on the lamination. This would give you the flexibility you need to adapt the material. Shapes could be used for most three-year-olds, for example, and letters for many four- and five-year-olds.

Marking on Writing Surfaces

Just as children enjoy using varied writing tools, they enjoy marking on varied surfaces. Many of these writing surfaces can be obtained at little or no expense. Examples include:

Newsprint
Computer paper
Construction paper (fade resistant)
Gift wrapping paper
Chalkboards
Audiovisual boards
Index cards
Sandpaper
Cardboard boxes
Shirt boxes
Tagboard sheets: colored and white

Working with Adhesives

Several types of adhesives are effective for preparing teacher made materials. Included are paste, a glue stick, regular glue, hot glue, and rubber cement. Paste is the least expensive adhesive source, but it is not always desirable. You may have difficulty spreading thin, even coats. Then, when the paste dries, you may find that the edges of the material curl. When used by the children, the curled edges may tear, resulting in a damaged or an unattractive piece of material.

Glue. Glue is an alternative. It is more effective than paste, but it is also more expensive. This prohibits many teachers and schools with restricted budgets from using it.

Glue Stick. A glue stick is a convenient tool for applying glue. Be careful to replace the cover after use to prevent drying.

Hot Glue Gun. The hot glue gun may be used effectively to construct materials from wood, fabric, and plastic. It is not necessary, however, for constructing many of the materials described in this book.

Choosing Lettering

Two lettering choices are available: computer generated or hand printed. Before preparing the materials, practice manuscript writing to ensure that the letters appear professional.

You may feel more comfortable using a soft lead pencil to sketch your letters first. Once you are satisfied with your letters, trace over them using a medium felt-tip marker.

Titling Materials

When used, the title should be used to describe the teaching material. The color used to create the title should complement the background paper, as well as objects pictured. Titles need to be created from strong colors and provide contrast. As a result, you will find that primary colors make interesting titles.

You may question the type of lettering—uppercase or lowercase—that should be used in preparing titles. Some teachers prefer to use uppercase letters when the title is not a complete sentence. For a complete sentence, they prefer capitalizing the first word. Also, they place a period at the end of the sentence. Examples include:

Incomplete Sentences	Complete Sentences
Writing	Draw your home.
My Home	You can write.
A Truck	Select a gift.
Water Animals	Write your name.
Our World	Choose a color.
Valentine's Day	Find the letters.

Making Materials

Whether you prepare the teacher materials in this book or design your own, the following suggestions will help:

- Select a large, clean area to prepare your materials.

- Collect supplies, including a tool set. Include such items as:
  Ruler, yardstick, and/or straight edge tool
  Scissors
  Soft lead pencils
  Glue, rubber cement, and/or paste
  Colored felt-tip markers
  Oil pastels
  Colored pencils

Selecting Coloring Media

One key to professional appearing materials is evenly applied color. To apply color evenly, choose the appropriate medium. Several media can be used. Oil pastels and watercolor markers are the most effective. While crayons can be used, teachers generally prefer the finished appearance of oil pastels and markers.

Preparing Patterns

The patterns used for the figures on teaching materials in this book may be prepared in several ways. You may have the skill to draw them freehand, but if you do not, you can choose patterns from coloring books or children's storybooks. Place these materials under an opaque or overhead projector and trace the designs, enlarging them, if necessary.

Using an Opaque Projector. The opaque projector is an excellent tool for people who lack drawing skill. To use this piece of equipment, place the picture that must be magnified on the tray. Then, tape a piece of tagboard or construction paper onto a wall or a door. Adjust the machine to obtain the figure size that is in proportion to your paper, bulletin board or chart, and other figures. Using a pencil, lightly trace the image onto the paper. If color is needed, it is easier to fill it in on a flat surface, such as a table or desk, after reproducing the object.

Using an Overhead Projector. Place a transparency of the figure on the glass plate, then tape a piece of tagboard, construction, or other type of paper on the wall. Turn the lamp on using the switch on the front of the projector. Adjust the size of the figure by moving the projector. For smaller figures, move the projector closer to the paper. For larger figures, move the projector farther from the paper.

Using Clip Art. Computer-generated clip art can be used for figures. Using a search engine, type in the words "clip art" to obtain different sites.

Storing Materials

For easy reference, store all theme-related materials in the same box or location. Proper storage enhances materials' longevity. Ideally, teacher made are stored in a dry, well-ventilated area. Small pieces of materials can be stored in envelopes, self-sealing transparent bags, manila folders, or boxes. Large charts should be stored on flat surfaces to avoid warping.

Caring for Materials

Durability is an important consideration when planning teacher made materials. Whenever possible, select heavy tagboard or construction paper. After constructing the material, laminate it. The plastic coating strengthens the materials and helps ensure many years of use.

Criteria for Evaluating Teacher Made Materials

	Needs Improvement	Acceptable	Commendable
1. Is the material developmentally appropriate?			
2. Is the material safe?			
3. Are the teaching criteria clear?			
4. Does the teacher made material enrich the classroom activity?			
5. Does the material stimulate curiosity and encourage interaction?			
6. Does the material promote developmental skills?			
7. Is the material relevant, projecting accurate and up-to-date concepts?			
8. Is the material of good design?			
9. Does the material actively involve the children?			
10. Is the material user-friendly?			
11. Is the material aesthetically pleasing?			
12. Can the material be adapted to other themes?			
13. Is the material anti-bias (cultural, age, gender)?			
14. Is the lettering accurate?			
15. Does the value to the children justify the time, effort, and expense (if any)?			

Art

Bead Necklace Chart

Developmental Goals

1. Develop an appreciation for the printed word.
2. Follow directions.
3. Create and extend a pattern.
4. Develop small muscle skills.
5. Develop eye-hand coordination skills.

Related Curriculum Themes

Colors	Jewelry
Patterns	Costumes
Shapes	Math

Curriculum Areas

Math	Language Arts
Art	

Preparation Tools and Materials

- One sheet of white tagboard
- Construction paper or sentence strips
- Markers
- Glue or hot glue gun
- Scissors
- String, yarn, or craft string
- Beads

Directions

1. Type or use a marker to print the title, supply list, and directions on construction paper or sentence strips.

   WHAT YOU NEED:
   - Beads
   - String

   WHAT TO DO:
   a. Choose a pattern.
   b. Holding onto one end, place a bead on the string.
   c. Continue placing beads until all beads are used.
   d. Tie both ends in a double knot.
   e. Wear!

2. Use glue to attach the title, supply list, and direction strips sequentially on the tagboard, leaving a few inches between the direction steps.

3. Use glue or a hot glue gun to attach the beads and string pieces to illustrate each step of the directions.

Make a Bead Necklace

What you need:
☆ beads   ☆ string

What to do:
(1) Decide on a pattern.

(2) Holding onto one end, place a bead onto the string.

(3) Continue placing beads until all beads are used.

(4) Tie both ends in a double knot.

(5) Wear!

Teaching/Learning Strategies

- Place the bead necklace chart near a table. Gather the necessary supplies and put them on the table. If desired, tie a knot at the end of the string to prevent beads from slipping off as children work. Children will need assistance with Step d, in which they tie a double knot to create the necklace. (*Note:* This activity is inappropriate for very young children due to the small size of the beads.)

Bubble Print Chart

Developmental Goals

1. Develop an appreciation for the printed word.
2. Develop an appreciation for art.
3. Develop color identification skills.
4. Experience a print-rich environment.
5. Follow directions.
6. Develop eye-hand coordination skills.
7. Develop small muscle skills.

Related Curriculum Themes

Water	Colors
Bubbles	Sight
Air	Our World

Curriculum Areas

Sensory	Art
Science	Language Arts
Math	

Preparation Tools and Materials

- One sheet of white tagboard
- Colored felt-tip markers
- Black construction paper
- Lamination paper

Bubble Prints

In a cup mix these ingredients:

½ cup   2 tbsp.   1 tbsp.

Place a straw in the cup.

Blow bubbles until they begin to overflow.

Remove straw and place paper over the bubbles.

Remove the paper from the bubbles.

Directions

1. On the sheet of tagboard, use the markers to print the following directions and draw the corresponding illustrations (see the accompanying photo):

   BUBBLE PRINTS
   a. In a cup, mix the following ingredients:
      ½ cup of water
      2 tablespoons liquid dish soap
      1 tablespoon food coloring
   b. Place a straw in the cup.
   c. Blow bubbles until they begin to overflow.
   d. Remove the straw and place paper over the bubbles.
   e. Remove the paper from the bubbles.

2. Laminate the chart.

Teaching/Learning Strategies

- Gather the materials needed to make bubble prints. Make sure to provide a variety of paper colors. Provide smocks and protective coverings for tables, and place the bubbles in the sensory, art, or science area. Before the activity, encourage the children to practice blowing air through a straw. Display the chart at the children's eye level.

Bubble Recipe Chart

Developmental Goals

1. Develop an appreciation for the printed word.
2. Develop observation skills.
3. Practice following directions.
4. Experience a print-rich environment.
5. Practice decoding symbols and written words.

Related Curriculum Themes

Water   Colors
Air   Our World
Bubbles

Curriculum Areas

Sensory   Language Arts
Science

Preparation Tools and Materials

- One sheet of white tagboard
- Colored felt-tip markers
- Lamination paper

Directions

1. On the sheet of tagboard, use the markers to print the following directions and draw the corresponding illustrations (see the accompanying photo):

   ### BUBBLE RECIPE
   a. In a bucket, mix the following ingredients:
      8 cups of water
      ¾ cup of liquid dish soap
      ¼ cup of glycerin
   b. Use the solution to make bubbles.

2. Laminate the chart.

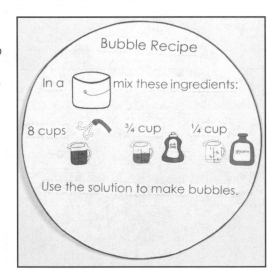

Teaching/Learning Strategies

- Following the directions on the chart, prepare the bubble solution with assistance from the children. Provide various bubble makers with the solution, such as plastic six-pack soda rings, pipe cleaners, plastic berry baskets, and commercial bubble rings.

- If the children have the prerequisite skills, let them read the chart.

Chunk Crayons

Developmental Goals

1. Learn the physical nature of materials.
2. Gain a sense of accomplishment and self-confidence.
3. Learn to appreciate the value of a marking tool.
4. Express feelings, explore, and experiment.
5. Develop small muscle coordination skills.
6. Learn to think in an original way.
7. Experience a print-rich environment.
8. Practice following a sequence.

Related Curriculum Themes

Colors	Tools
Art	Communication
Pictures	Crayons

Curriculum Areas

Art	Science
Small Motor	

Preparation Tools and Materials

- One sheet of tagboard
- Construction paper or sentence strips
- Markers
- Glue or glue stick
- Scissors (optional: craft scissors)
- Lamination paper

Chunk Crayons

(1) Turn the oven on and set it to 300°.

(2) Place crayon pieces in the muffin tin.

(3) Place the tin in the oven, carefully monitoring the melting process.

(4) Remove the warm, melted crayons from the muffin tin.

(5) Cool until set and remove from tin.

Directions

1. Type or use a marker to print the following title and procedures on construction paper or sentence strips (see the accompanying photo):

   CHUNK CRAYONS
   a. Turn the oven on to 300°.
   b. Place crayon pieces in the muffin tin.
   c. Place the tin in the oven, carefully monitoring the melting process.
   d. Remove the warm, melted crayons from the muffin tin.
   e. Cool until set and remove from tin.

2. Use scissors to cut the strips apart.

3. Use glue to attach the title and direction strips sequentially on the piece of tagboard.

4. Laminate the chart.

Teaching/Learning Strategies

- Before undertaking this activity, collect broken or discarded crayons. Remove paper wrappings from the crayon pieces. With the children, use the chart to create chunk crayons.

- Prepare both single-color and multi-colored chunk crayons. (*Hint:* When making multi-colored crayons, remove them from the oven before pieces totally melt together and turn brown.)

- Once cooled, encourage the children to use the chunk crayons in the art area.

Clown Makeup Chart

Developmental Goals

1. Experiment and discover new ways of using materials.
2. Develop eye-hand coordination skills.
3. Develop color-identification skills.
4. Develop skills in creative expression.
5. Develop an awareness of changes in substance.
6. Develop an appreciation for the printed word.
7. Practice following directions.

Related Curriculum Themes

Circus	Art
Clowns	Feelings
Halloween	Colors

Curriculum Areas

Dramatic Play	Science
Art	

Preparation Tools and Materials

- One sheet of tagboard
- Construction paper
- Markers
- Scissors
- Glue or glue stick
- Lamination paper

Directions

1. On a sheet of tagboard, use a watercolor marker to print the following recipe and draw the corresponding illustrations (see the accompanying photo):

   CLOWN MAKEUP
   a. For each color of makeup, mix these ingredients in a bowl:
      3 to 5 drops of food coloring
      ¼ cup of cold cream
   b. Apply makeup by hand or with a clean paintbrush.

2. Laminate the chart.

Teaching/Learning Strategies

- Provide plenty of time for the children to experiment with the cause-and-effect relationship of preparing the makeup. Young children learn by doing.

- Once the makeup is prepared, provide mirrors and paintbrushes so the child can apply the makeup. Some children will prefer applying the makeup with their hands; others will use a brush. To remove the makeup, provide washcloths, soap, and water.

Crayon and Marker Bundles Chart

Developmental Goals

1. Experiment with art media.
2. Develop small motor coordination skills.
3. Practice following directions.
4. Experiment with cause-and-effect relationships.
5. Develop an appreciation for the printed word.

Related Curriculum Themes

Colors   Communication
Art   Crayons
Tools

Curriculum Areas

Art
Small Motor

Preparation Tools and Materials

- One sheet of tagboard
- Construction paper or sentence strips

- Markers
- Scissors
- Glue or glue stick
- Lamination paper

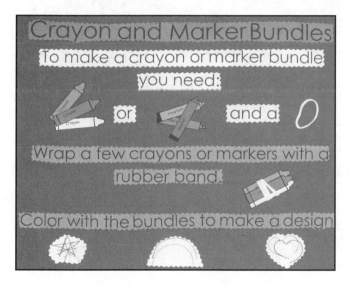

Directions

1. On a sheet of tagboard, use a watercolor marker to print the following directions and draw the corresponding illustrations for making crayon or marker bundles (see the accompanying photo):

   ### CRAYON AND MARKER BUNDLES

   a. To make a crayon or marker bundle, you need:
      Crayons or markers
      Rubber bands
   b. Wrap a few crayons or markers with a rubber band.
   c. Color with the bundle to make a design.

2. Laminate the chart.

Teaching/Learning Strategies

- Place the chart at the children's eye level.

- Give the children paper so they can experiment with using the crayon bundles as marking tools.

- If desired, vary the art activity by making bundles of fewer or more crayons or markers and by changing the color combinations.

Crayon Identification Match

Developmental Goals

1. Develop color recognition skills.
2. Associate the printed word with a color.
3. Learn there is a Spanish word for a color.
4. Experience a print-rich environment.
5. Develop visual discrimination skills.

Related Curriculum Themes

Art   Writing Tools
Colors   Words

Curriculum Area

Language Arts

Preparation Tools and Materials

- Tagboard (blue, green, yellow, red, white, pink, and orange)
- Black marker
- Ruler
- Scissors
- Glue
- Lamination paper

Directions

1. Measure and cut two 18″ x 7″ crayons out of each color of tagboard.

2. On one side of each crayon, print the English word for the color. On the other side, print the English and the Spanish word.

3. Laminate all pieces.

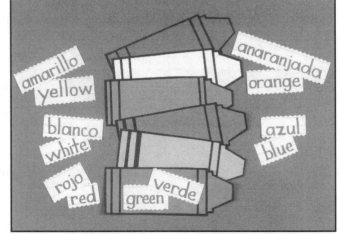

Teaching/Learning Strategies

- During group time, share the crayons with the children by introducing the English and Spanish word for each color. Then, place one set of crayons on the classroom bulletin board or on a wall at the children's eye level. Using both sets, the children can match the colors.

- Extend the activity, if developmentally appropriate, by including such colors as gray, teal, lime, gold, and silver.

Fingerpainting in a Bag

Developmental Goals

1. Develop creative expression.
2. Develop color identification skills.
3. Learn to mix colors.
4. Develop small muscle coordination skills.
5. Develop eye-hand coordination skills.

Related Curriculum Themes

Art   Painting
Colors

Curriculum Areas

Sensory   Science
Art   Small Motor

Preparation Tools and Materials

- Gallon size self-sealing plastic bags
- Masking tape
- Tempera or fingerpaint

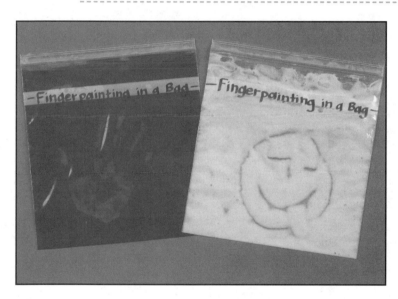

Directions

1. Place ¼ cup of fingerpaint in each bag.

2. Seal the bag, adding masking tape along the edge for extra protection.

Teaching/Learning Strategies

- Place the bags of fingerpaint on a table. If needed, show the children how to use the bag.

- This activity can be extended by placing two colors of tempera paint in a bag and encouraging the children to mix them. Avoid using sharp objects on the bag. This could create holes in the bag.

Goop Recipe Chart

Developmental Goals

1. Develop tactile awareness.
2. Observe the changes in a substance.
3. Develop small muscle coordination skills.
4. Develop an appreciation for the printed word.
5. Practice following directions.
6. Recognize that the spoken word can be represented in print.
7. Develop left-to-right progression skills.

Related Curriculum Themes

Touch   Recipes
Colors

Curriculum Areas

Sensory   Language Arts
Science

Preparation Tools and Materials

- One sheet of white tagboard
- Colored felt-tip markers
- Lamination paper

Directions

1. On the sheet of tagboard, use the markers to print the following directions and draw the corresponding illustrations (see the accompanying photo):

   GOOP RECIPE
   a. Pour 2" of cornstarch into the container.
   b. Add 4 drops of food coloring.
   c. Slowly add and stir enough water to make a thick mixture.
   d. Enjoy playing with the goop, using your fingers, spoons, bowls, and strainers.

2. Laminate the chart.

Teaching/Learning Strategies

- Gather the needed materials and display the chart at the children's eye level. Allow the children to help you prepare the goop. Refer to the chart, following the directions. If the children have the prerequisite skills, let them read the chart.

- Tools like small plastic rakes, scoops, and bottles can be used with the goop to extend the activity.

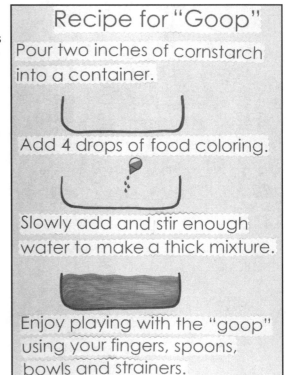

Recipe for "Goop"

Pour two inches of cornstarch into a container.

Add 4 drops of food coloring.

Slowly add and stir enough water to make a thick mixture.

Enjoy playing with the "goop" using your fingers, spoons, bowls and strainers.

Silly Clay

Developmental Goals

1. Sensually explore materials.
2. Practice following directions.
3. Develop sensory awareness skills.

Related Curriculum Themes

Senses   Shapes
Cooking   Sensory Modeling
Measuring   Mediums
I'm Me, I'm   Colors
  Special

Curriculum Areas

Art   Math
Reading
  Readiness

Preparation Tools and Materials

- One sheet of 22" x 28" tagboard
- Construction paper or sentence strips
- Watercolor markers
- Ruler
- Glue or glue stick
- Lamination paper

Silly Clay

Ingredients:

1 cup liquid starch

2 cups white glue

Mix all ingredients in a bowl.

Knead with hands until smooth.

Food coloring may be added.

Store in container.

Directions

1. Draw a picture to illustrate each step in making silly clay on the tagboard (see the accompanying photo). Include:

   - Liquid starch bottle and one measuring cup
   - Glue bottle and two measuring cups
   - Starch bottle and glue bottle with arrows pointing to mixing bowl (a hand stirring the contents with the spoon)
   - Two hands kneading bowl contents
   - Bottle of food coloring dripping into the bowl
   - Airtight, covered storage container

2. Type or use a marker to print the following title and directions on construction paper or sentence strips (see the accompanying photo):

   #### SILLY CLAY INGREDIENTS

   - 1 cup liquid starch
   - 2 cups white glue
   - Mix all ingredients in a bowl.
   - Knead the mixture with your hands until it is smooth.
   - Add food coloring, if desired.
   - Store in a covered container.

3. Use glue or a glue stick to attach the title, directions, and illustrations to the tagboard sheet.

4. Laminate the chart.

Teaching/Learning Strategies

- Add different colors to the clay depending on the holiday season or theme.

- Provide the children with cookie cutters, rolling pins, and plastic knives.

- After the children have finished playing with the medium, place it in a covered container in the refrigerator to preserve it temporarily.

Snowflake Chart

Developmental Goals

1. Develop eye-hand coordination skills.
2. Develop small motor skills.
3. Develop aesthetic appreciation.
4. Practice following directions.
5. Develop right-to-left progression skills.
6. Develop visual perception skills.

Related Curriculum Themes

Winter   Paper
Weather   Scissors

Curriculum Areas

Small Motor   Art

Preparation Tools and Materials

- One sheet of light blue tagboard
- Six pieces of 5" x 5" white construction paper
- Black felt-tip marker
- Ruler
- Glue or glue stick
- Lamination paper
- Scissors

Directions

1. Print the words "Make a Snowflake" across the top of the tagboard sheet.

2. Using a ruler and a black felt-tip marker, draw six 11" x 8" rectangles on the remaining space of the tagboard (see the accompanying photo).

3. Number each rectangle sequentially, as illustrated.

4. In the first rectangle, glue one of the white squares.

5. For the second rectangle, fold one of the white squares in half. Glue one-half to the tagboard.

6. Fold another white square in half vertically. You will then have a rectangle. Fold up the bottom third and glue the back to the third rectangle so the last fold shows.

7. Take another white square and repeat the folds in Steps 5 and 6. Then, fold down the top third and glue the back to the fourth rectangle.

8. Take another square and repeat the folds in Steps 5, 6, and 7. Cut this piece with scissors as you would to make a snowflake and glue it, still folded, to the fifth rectangle.

9. Take the last square and repeat the folds in Steps 5, 6, and 7, and make the cuts as outlined in Step 8. Unfold the completed snowflake and glue it to the sixth rectangle.

10. Laminate the chart.

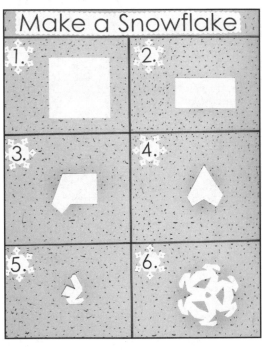

Teaching/Learning Strategies

- Self-directed art activities should be available daily. Display the snowflake chart in the art area with paper and child-size scissors to encourage student involvement. If desired, encourage the children to attach their snowflakes to a bulletin board with the title "Snowflakes."

Squeeze Bottle Art Chart

Developmental Goals

1. Develop small muscle skills.
2. Experiment with art media.
3. Observe changes in substances.
4. Develop pride in personal creativity.
5. Develop an appreciation for the printed word.
6. Develop left-to-right progression skills.
7. Practice following directions.

Related Curriculum Themes

Art   Print
Colors   Communication
Containers

Curriculum Areas

Art   Science
Language Arts   Math

Preparation Tools and Materials

- One sheet of tagboard
- Felt-tip markers
- Glue or glue stick
- Scissors
- Lamination paper

Squeeze Bottle Art

For each color of squeeze bottle art, mix these ingredients in a bowl:

½ cup

flour

½ cup

or

salt

½ cup

Pour the mixture into a

Squeeze the bottle onto paper or cardboard to create a design.

Directions

1. On a sheet of tagboard, use a watercolor marker to print the following recipe and draw the corresponding illustrations (see the accompanying photo):

   SQUEEZE BOTTLE ART
   a. For each color of squeeze bottle art, mix these ingredients in a bowl:
      ½ cup of water
      ½ cup of flour
      ½ cup of salt
      2 teaspoons of powdered tempera paint or food coloring
   b. Pour the mixture into an empty, plastic squeeze bottle.
   c. Squeeze the bottle onto paper or cardboard, creating a design.

2. Laminate the chart.

Teaching/Learning Strategies

- Assemble the ingredients on the chart. Encourage the children to help mix the paint.

- Younger children may enjoy using the mixture for fingerpainting.

Classroom Environment

Birthday Cakes

Developmental Goals

1. Experience a print-rich environment.
2. Develop an appreciation for the printed word.
3. Develop an understanding of birthday celebrations.
4. Recognize that the spoken word can be represented in print.
5. Recognize one's name in print.
6. Associate birthdays with months and dates.

Related Curriculum Themes

Birthdays   Symbols
Special Days   Alphabet Letters
Foods   Numerals

Curriculum Areas

Language Arts
Social Studies

Preparation Tools and Materials

- Four sheets of white tagboard
- Black felt-tip marker
- Watercolor markers
- Scissors (craft scissors optional)
- Glue or glue stick
- Lamination paper

Directions

1. Using a black felt-tip marker, draw 12 8" x 12" birthday cakes on the white tagboard.

2. Cut out the cakes, and decorate them with the watercolor markers.

3. Type or print the name of each month on a cake (see the accompanying photo).

4. Laminate the cake pieces.

5. Using a watercolor marker, print each child's name and birthday on the appropriate cake.

Teaching/Learning Strategies

- If developmentally appropriate, the children can print their names and dates of birth on the cakes representing the months of their births.

- Hang the birthday cakes in the classroom, or adhere them to a bulletin board. At the beginning of each month, use the charts to review the birthdays.

Birthday Packages

Developmental Goals

1. Experience a print-rich environment.
2. Develop an appreciation for the printed word.
3. Develop an understanding of social customs.
4. Recognize that the spoken word can be represented in print.
5. Recognize one's name in print.
6. Associate birthdays with months and dates.

Related Curriculum Themes

Birthdays   Alphabet Letters
Special Days   Symbols
Self-Concept   Numerals

Curriculum Areas

Language Arts
Social Studies

Preparation Tools and Materials

- Twelve sheets of construction, craft, or wrapping paper, 12" x 18"
- Black felt tip marker
- Watercolor markers
- Scissors (decorative craft scissors optional)
- Lamination paper

Directions

1. Using a black felt-tip marker, draw a gift package design on each of the 12 sheets of the paper (see the accompanying photo).

2. Cut out the gift packages, and decorate them with the watercolor markers.

3. Type or use a marker to print the name of each month on a package.

4. Laminate the pieces.

5. Using a watercolor marker, print each child's name and birthday on the appropriate package.

Teaching/Learning Strategies

- If the children have the prerequisite skills, they can print their names on the packages identifying the months of their births.

- Hang the birthday packages in the room, or attach them to a bulletin board. Refer to them during large group time to identify the months and dates of children's birthdays.

Birthday Train

Classroom Environment

Developmental Goals

1. Experience a print-rich environment.
2. Develop an appreciation for the printed word.
3. Develop an understanding of social customs.
4. Recognize that the spoken word can be represented in print.
5. Recognize one's name in print.
6. Associate birthdays with months and dates.

Related Curriculum Themes

Birthdays	Alphabet Letters
Self-Concept	Numerals
Special Days	Symbols

Curriculum Area

Language Arts

Preparation Tools and Materials

- Thirteen sheets of colored construction paper, 12" x 18"
- Black felt-tip marker
- Watercolor markers
- Glue or glue stick
- Lamination paper

Directions

1. Using a black felt-tip marker, draw a train engine and 12 cars on individual sheets of colored construction paper (see the accompanying photo).

2. Cut out the engine and cars.

3. Use the glue or glue stick to attach the wheels.

4. Use the colored markers to add detail.

5. Type or print the words "Birthday Train" on the engine.

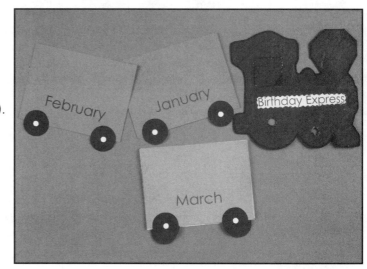

6. Type or print the name of each month on a train car.

7. Laminate the train pieces.

8. Using a watercolor marker, type or print each child's name and birthday on the appropriate train car.

Teaching/Learning Strategies

- Display the train in the room at the children's eye level.
- Announce the birthdays at the beginning of each month and then again on the children's birthdays.

Book Return Box

Developmental Goals

1. Practice returning books.
2. Develop an appreciation for the printed word.
3. Learn the library usage routine.
4. Develop a sense of responsibility for using library books.

Related Curriculum Themes

Books　　　　Containers
Libraries　　　Our School
Alphabet Letters

Curriculum Areas

Language Arts
Social Studies

Preparation Tools and Materials

- One cardboard box, 15" x 10"
- Lamination paper
- Colored contact paper
- Black, felt-tip, permanent marker
- Scissors (craft scissors optional)

Directions

1. Apply the colored contact paper to the box.
2. Using a marker, type or print the title "Book Return" on the box.

Teaching/Learning Strategies

- For programs that include a lending library for parents and children, place the book return in an area that is convenient for both. Otherwise, place the box in the reading area of the classroom.

Clock Decorations

Developmental Goals

1. Develop object-identification skills.
2. Develop aesthetic appreciation.
3. Develop color-recognition skills.
4. Learn about seasonal symbols.

Related Curriculum Themes

Seasons   Holidays
Can Be Adapted to Any Theme

Curriculum Areas

Room Environment
Language Arts

Preparation Tools and Materials

- One sheet of tag-board for each clock decoration
- Colored felt-tip markers
- Scissors (craft scissors optional)
- Ruler or tape measure
- Pencil
- Lamination paper

Directions

1. With a ruler or tape measure, measure the face of your clock.

2. Using a pencil, draw a circle of equal diameter on the tagboard.

3. Choose a seasonal symbol from the following list, or develop one of your own and sketch it in pencil around the circle (see the accompanying photo).

   Symbols for each month might include the following:

   January—Mitten
   February—Heart
   March—Kite or shamrock
   April—Umbrella or bunny
   May—Flower
   June—Sun
   July—Ice cream cone
   August—Watermelon
   September—Apple
   October—Pumpkin
   November—Turkey
   December—Decorated tree

4. With a felt-tip marker, trace over the pencil marks and decorate and color the symbol as desired with additional markers.

5. Cut out the circle, providing a frame for the face of the clock.

6. Cover the tagboard with lamination paper.

Teaching/Learning Strategies

- During each month, season, or holiday, display a decoration on the classroom clock.

Labels for Classroom Areas or Centers

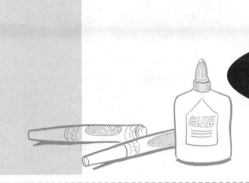

Developmental Goals

1. Develop visual-discrimination skills.
2. Develop letter-recognition skills.
3. Experience a print-rich environment.
4. Develop language skills.
5. Recognize that the spoken word can be represented in print.
6. Develop literacy skills.

Related Curriculum Themes

Art   Signs
Music   Our School
Books   Communication

Curriculum Area

Language Arts

Preparation Tools and Materials

- Tagboard and/or sentence strips
- Pictures depicting classroom areas (from educational-supply catalogs)
- Black felt-tip marker
- Scissors (craft scissors optional)
- Glue or glue stick
- Lamination paper

Directions

1. Cut out one tagboard piece, approximately 10" x 9", or use a sentence strip for each classroom area or center (e.g., block building, art, storytelling, math, music, science, dramatic play, bathroom, computer).

2. From educational-supply catalogs, cut out pictures depicting areas or centers.

3. Glue different pictures onto each tagboard piece or sentence strip. For example, the art center label may contain pictures of markers, scissors, paint, glue, and crayons (see the accompanying photo).

4. Type or print the name of the area on each label.

5. Laminate all pieces.

Teaching/Learning Strategies

- Place the labels in the appropriate areas of the classroom. Point out the labels to the children, and ask them to guess the words written on them.

- Also consider placing the labels in the writing center. Let the children trace over the alphabet letters with grease pencils or watercolor markers.

Lost and Found Box

Developmental Goals

1. Develop a sense of responsibility for belongings.
2. Develop an appreciation for the printed word.
3. Learn the routine for lost-and-found objects.

Related Curriculum Themes

Boxes
Alphabet Letters
Our School

Curriculum Areas

Social Studies
Language Arts

Preparation Tools and Materials

- Cardboard box, with lid
- Colored contact paper
- Construction paper
- Colored felt-tip markers
- Scissors (craft scissors optional)
- Tape

Directions

1. Cover the box and lid with the colored contact paper.

2. Using felt-tip markers, print the words "Lost and Found" on a rectangular piece of construction paper.

3. Tape the label to the box lid.

Teaching/Learning Strategies

- The lost-and-found box can be placed near the classroom entrance for parents and children to look through for misplaced items.

Number of Children in Center Areas

Developmental Goals

1. Develop counting skills.
2. Become aware of classroom limits.
3. Develop an appreciation for printed words.
4. Recognize that the spoken word can be represented in print.

Related Curriculum Themes

School
Friends

Curriculum Areas

Language Arts
Math

Preparation Tools and Materials

- Tagboard
- Construction paper
- Scissors
- Glue or glue stick
- Markers
- Lamination paper

Directions

1. Cut the tagboard into 9" x 12" pieces.

2. Type or use a marker to print the name of a classroom center or area across the top of each tagboard piece.

3. Cut people shapes out of construction paper. If desired, add facial features.

4. Determine the maximum number of children for each classroom center or area.

5. Using glue or a glue stick, attach the corresponding number of people shapes to each center sign. For example, if you want to allow four children in the dramatic play area, glue four people shapes to the dramatic play area chart.

6. Laminate all signs.

Teaching/Learning Strategies

- Introduce the center signs in a large group setting. Explain the people shapes. Have the children count the people shapes on each sign. Allow the children to help place the charts in the classroom centers or areas.

Schedule Chart–Afternoon

Developmental Goals

1. Develop a sense of time.
2. Identify activities that occur in the afternoon.
3. Become familiar with classroom routines.
4. Develop an appreciation for the printed word.
5. Recognize that the spoken word can be represented in print.

Related Curriculum Themes

School   Alphabet Letters
Friends

Curriculum Areas

Language Arts
Math

Preparation Tools and Materials

- Sheet of white tagboard
- Construction paper or sentence strips
- Markers
- Scissors (craft scissors optional)
- Glue or glue stick
- Pictures cut from school-supply catalogs
- Lamination paper

Directions

1. Type or use a marker to print the caption "Our Afternoon Schedule" on construction paper or a sentence strip.

2. Using glue or a glue stick, attach the caption to the top portion of the tagboard.

3. Cut pictures from school-supply catalogs that depict activities that occur in the afternoon in your classroom. Some examples include rest time, self-selection, snack time, large group, and outdoor play.

4. Type or print the times of day and activity names on construction paper or sentence strips.

5. Using glue or a glue stick, attach the time cards, pictures, and activity names sequentially, on the tagboard (see the accompanying photo).

6. Laminate the chart.

Our Afternoon Schedule	
12:30	rest time
1:30	self-selection
2:15	snack
2:45	large group
3:30	outdoor play
4:00	self-selection

Teaching/Learning Strategies

- Hang the afternoon schedule chart on a classroom wall. During group time, refer to the chart to help notify the children of daily activities.

Schedule Chart–Morning

Developmental Goals

1. Develop a sense of time.
2. Identify activities that occur in the morning.
3. Become familiar with classroom routines.
4. Develop an appreciation for the printed word.
5. Recognize that the spoken word can be represented in print.

Classroom Environment

Related Curriculum Themes
School   Friends
Alphabet Letters

Curriculum Areas
Language Arts
Math

Preparation Tools and Materials

- One sheet of white tagboard
- Construction paper or sentence strips
- Markers
- Scissors (craft scissors optional)
- Glue or glue stick
- Pictures cut from school-supply catalogs
- Lamination paper

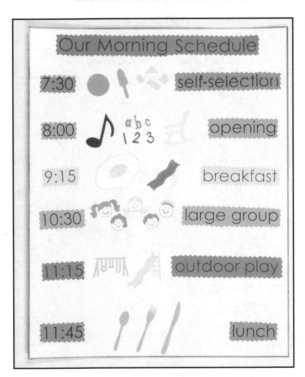

Directions

1. Type or use a marker to print the caption "Our Morning Schedule" on construction paper or a sentence strip.

2. Using glue or a glue stick, attach the caption to the top portion of the tagboard.

3. Cut pictures from school-supply catalogs that depict activities that occur in the morning in your classroom. Some examples include self-selection, opening/calendar time, breakfast, group time, outdoor play, and lunch.

4. Type or print the times of day and activity names on construction paper or sentence strips.

5. Using glue or a glue stick, attach the time cards, pictures, and activity names sequentially on the tagboard (see the accompanying photo).

6. Laminate the chart.

Teaching/Learning Strategies

- Hang the morning schedule chart next to the afternoon schedule chart on a classroom wall. Refer to the chart to help notify the children of daily activities.

Twinkle, Twinkle Traffic Light Chart

Classroom Environment

Developmental Goals

1. Identify traffic and safety signs.
2. Develop an enjoyment of music and songs.
3. Develop an appreciation for printed words.
4. Identify rhyming words.
5. Recognize that the spoken word can be represented in print.

Related Curriculum Themes

Safety	Wheels
Cars, Trucks, and Buses	Colors

Curriculum Areas

Social Studies	Language Arts
Health	Music

Preparation Tools and Materials

- One sheet of white tagboard
- Red, yellow, and green construction paper
- Markers
- Lamination paper
- White construction paper or sentence strips
- Scissors (craft scissors optional)
- Glue or glue stick

Directions

1. Draw a large traffic signal sign on the sheet of white tagboard (see the accompanying photo).

2. Cut a red, yellow, and green 6" circle out of construction paper.

3. Using glue or a glue stick, attach the circles vertically to the tagboard (red on top, yellow in the middle, green on the bottom).

4. Type or print the following song words on white construction paper or sentence strips:

   "Twinkle, Twinkle Traffic Light"
   Twinkle, twinkle traffic light,
   Standing on the corner bright.
   Green means go, we all know.
   Yellow means wait, even if you're late.
   Red means STOP!
   (Pause)
   Twinkle, twinkle traffic light,
   Standing on the corner bright.

5. Using glue or a glue stick, attach the song words to the chart.

6. Laminate the chart.

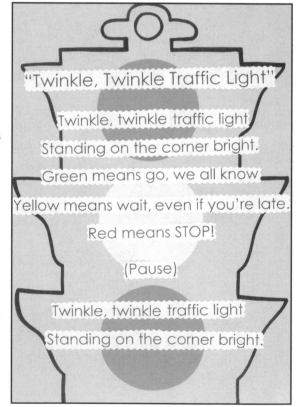

"Twinkle, Twinkle Traffic Light"

Twinkle, twinkle traffic light
Standing on the corner bright.
Green means go, we all know
Yellow means wait, even if you're late.
Red means STOP!

(Pause)

Twinkle, twinkle traffic light
Standing on the corner bright.

Teaching/Learning Strategies

- Introduce the chart and song in a large group setting, pointing to the colors as they are mentioned in the song. Encourage the children to sing the song with you. Set the chart out during free choice time for the children to use individually or in small groups.

Dramatic Play

Can Puppets

Dramatic Play

Developmental Goals

1. Develop expressive language skills.
2. Practice role playing.
3. Retell a story.

Related Curriculum Themes

Puppets   Communication
Friends   Containers

Curriculum Areas

Language Arts
Social Studies

Preparation Tools and Materials

- Clean, empty cans (soup-can size)
- Felt or fabric scraps
- Yarn
- Craft wiggle eyes (optional)
- Glue
- Cotton balls or pom poms

Directions

1. For each puppet, check that the can lacks sharp edges.

2. Cover a can with colored felt or fabric.

3. Using glue, attach features cut from felt, such as eyes, nose, mouth, and ears.

4. If desired, cut pieces of yarn and glue them to the can to represent hair.

5. If desired, use felt to create a hat for the puppet.

6. If desired, glue on craft wiggle eyes for the puppet's eyes.

7. Allow the cans to dry completely before using.

Teaching/Learning Strategies

- Place the can puppets in the book or dramatic play area of the classroom. Encourage the children to use them to retell a story or to conduct their own skit.

- These puppets can also be made using digital pictures of the children in your classroom.

Dramatic Play Menus

Developmental Goals

1. Develop an appreciation for printed words.
2. Practice role playing.
3. Identify breakfast, lunch, and dinner foods.
4. Develop visual discrimination skills.

Related Curriculum Themes

Foods   Families
Cooking   Occupations

Curriculum Areas

Social Studies
Language Arts

Preparation Tools and Materials

- Tagboard
- Markers
- Construction paper
- Scissors
- Glue
- Lamination paper
- Clip art pictures, stickers, or magazine photos (optional)

Directions

1. If using tagboard, cut into 9" x 12" pieces.

2. Draw breakfast items, such as eggs and bacon or cereal, on one piece of tagboard. Label it "Breakfast Menu."

3. On the back of the breakfast menu, type or use a marker to print a list of breakfast items and prices.

4. Create lunch and dinner menus by repeating Steps 2 and 3.

5. If desired, use clip art or magazine photos of food items in the menus.

6. Laminate all menus.

Teaching/Learning Strategies

- Place the menus in the dramatic play area with such additional props as aprons, pads of paper, pencils, a cash register, tablecloths, plastic vases of flowers, dishes, and pretend food items. Encourage the children to take turns ordering food from the menus.

Dramatic Play Sign—Apple Stand

Developmental Goals

1. Develop an appreciation for the printed word.
2. Practice role playing.
3. Develop expressive language skills.
4. Develop prosocial behaviors.

Dramatic Play

Related Curriculum Themes

Apples   Foods
Fruits   Fall
Red

Curriculum Areas

Social Studies
Language Arts

Preparation Tools and Materials

- One sheet of green tagboard
- Red, yellow, and green construction paper

- Markers
- Scissors
- Glue or glue stick
- Alphabet stencils
- Lamination paper

Directions

1. Using alphabet stencils and scissors, trace and cut from construction paper the letters of the words "Apple Stand."

2. Draw and cut from red, yellow, or green construction paper apple shapes.

3. Using glue or a glue stick, attach the words and apple shapes to the tagboard.

4. Laminate the tagboard.

Teaching/Learning Strategies

- Place the apple stand sign in the dramatic play area. Provide additional props, such as a cash register, play money, purses, wallets, apples (real or play), bags, bushel barrels, and pictures or posters of apples. Encourage the children to pretend to buy and sell apples.

Dramatic Play Sign–Campground

Developmental Goals

1. Develop an appreciation for the printed word.
2. Practice role playing.
3. Develop expressive language skills.
4. Develop prosocial behaviors.

Related Curriculum Themes

Camping   Family
Summer   Friends
Vacations

Curriculum Areas

Social Studies
Language Arts

Preparation Tools and Materials

- One sheet of tagboard
- Construction paper
- Markers
- Scissors (craft scissors optional)
- Glue or glue stick
- Alphabet stencils
- Clip art (optional)
- Lamination paper

Directions

1. Using alphabet stencils and scissors, trace and cut from construction paper the letters of the word "Campground."

2. If desired, use scissors to round off the top portion of the tagboard.

3. Using glue or a glue stick, attach the letters to the upper portion of the tagboard.

4. Use clip art or draw such campground items as tents, campfire, and lanterns on the tagboard.

5. Laminate the sign.

Teaching/Learning Strategies

- Place the campground sign in the dramatic play area. Provide additional camping props, such as a small tent, sleeping bags, pillows, flashlights, logs to represent a campfire, a cooler, and pictures or posters of trees and woodland areas. Encourage the children to take a pretend camping trip.

Dramatic Play Sign–Class Store

Dramatic Play

Developmental Goals

1. Develop an appreciation for the printed word.
2. Practice role playing.
3. Develop expressive language skills.
4. Develop prosocial behaviors.

Related Curriculum Themes

School   Grocery Store
Food

Curriculum Areas

Social Studies
Language Arts

Preparation Tools and Materials

- One sheet of tagboard
- Construction paper
- Pencil
- Scissors
- Glue or glue stick
- Alphabet stencils
- Lamination paper

Directions

1. Using alphabet stencils and scissors, trace and cut from construction paper the letters of the words "Class Store."
2. Using glue or a glue stick, attach the words to the tagboard.
3. Laminate the sign.

Teaching/Learning Strategies

- Place the class store sign in the dramatic play area. Provide additional props, such as a cash register, play money, purses, wallets, empty cereal and food boxes, empty and clean dairy product containers, empty and clean food cans, and pictures and posters of foods. Encourage the children to "go to the store."

Dramatic Play Sign—Hospital

Developmental Goals

1. Develop an appreciation for the printed word.
2. Practice role playing.
3. Develop expressive language skills.
4. Recognize that the spoken word can be represented in print.

Related Curriculum Themes

Doctors and Nurses   Friends
Hospital   Family
Occupations

Curriculum Areas

Social Studies   Language Arts
Health

Preparation Tools and Materials

- One sheet of tagboard
- Construction paper (or hospital-related wrapping paper, if available)

- Scissors
- Glue or glue stick
- Alphabet stencils
- Bandages (optional)
- Lamination paper

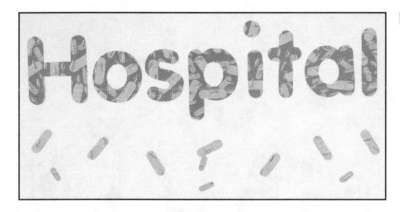

Directions

1. Using alphabet stencils and scissors, trace and cut from construction paper or hospital-related wrapping paper the letters of the word "Hospital."

2. Using glue or a glue stick, attach the letters to the tagboard.

3. If desired, decorate the tagboard with bandages or cutouts from wrapping paper.

4. Laminate the sign.

Teaching/Learning Strategies

- Place the hospital sign in the dramatic play area. Provide additional hospital props, such as cots, doctor and nurse clothing, stethoscopes, bandages, bandage wraps, x-ray pictures, pretend syringes, and pictures or posters related to health. Encourage the children to play in the area.

Dramatic Play Sign—Paint Store

Developmental Goals

1. Develop an appreciation for the printed word.
2. Practice role playing.
3. Develop expressive language skills.
4. Develop prosocial behaviors.

Related Curriculum Themes

Colors   Occupations
Art   Brushes

Curriculum Areas

Social Studies
Language Arts

Preparation Tools and Materials

- One sheet of white tagboard
- Construction paper
- Scissors
- Markers
- Glue or glue stick
- Alphabet stencils
- Lamination paper

Directions

1. Using alphabet stencils and scissors, trace and cut from various colors of construction paper the letters of the words "Paint Store."

2. Using glue or a glue stick, attach the words to the tagboard.

3. Using markers, draw paint supplies on the sign, such as a paint bucket, paint brushes, and a paint pallet (see the accompanying photo).

4. Laminate the sign.

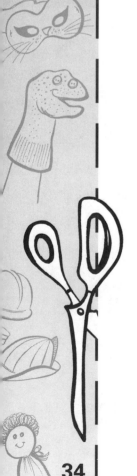

Teaching/Learning Strategies

- Place the paint store sign in the dramatic play area. Provide additional props to be used in the paint store, including a cash register, play money, purses, wallets, empty paint cans, brushes and rollers, stir sticks, painters' caps, wallpaper sample books, and paint chip sample cards. Encourage the children to pretend to buy and sell painting supplies.

Duck Stick Puppets

Developmental Goals

1. Practice role playing.
2. Develop expressive language.
3. Practice counting.
4. Develop eye-hand coordination skills.

Related Curriculum Themes

Birds   Music
Puppets   Nursery Rhymes
Farm

Curriculum Areas

Language Arts
Music

Preparation Tools and Materials

- Tagboard or construction paper
- Markers or crayons
- Scissors
- Glue or tape
- Craft sticks
- Lamination paper

Dramatic Play

Directions

1. Using markers or crayons, draw duck shapes on the tagboard or construction paper (see the accompanying photo).

2. Decorate the ducks as desired, and cut out the duck shapes.

3. Laminate all pieces.

4. Using glue or tape, attach the duck shapes to craft sticks.

Teaching/Learning Strategies

- Use the duck stick puppets as props to introduce a book or song about ducks. Then, place the puppets near the book corner or dramatic play area for the children's use. When appropriate, the children can prepare their own stick puppets.

Egg Carton Puppets

Developmental Goals

1. Develop expressive language skills.
2. Experiment and discover new ways of using materials.
3. Develop small motor coordination skills.
4. Develop eye-hand coordination skills.
5. Practice expressing feelings.

Related Curriculum Themes

Puppets   Feelings
Communication

Curriculum Areas

Language Arts
Social Studies

Preparation Tools and Materials

- Egg cartons
- Adult socks
- Scissors
- Craft pom-poms
- Moveable plastic eyes
- Craft glue or hot glue gun
- Contact paper scraps

Directions

1. Using scissors, cut the egg carton in half.
2. Cut off the toe of a sock, and glue the sock opening to the egg carton (see the accompanying photo).
3. Decorate the puppet with contact paper scraps, pom-poms, and eyes.

Teaching/Learning Strategies

- This activity can also be extended for older children by giving those children the materials to make their own puppets.

- Give the children a mirror and/or a puppet stage for conducting puppet shows.

Goldilocks and the Three Bears Props

Developmental Goals

1. Practice role playing.
2. Practice retelling a story.
3. Develop expressive language skills.
4. Develop prosocial behaviors.

Related Curriculum Themes
Books   Make Believe
Bears   Communication
Storytelling

Curriculum Areas
Language Arts
Social Studies

Preparation Tools and Materials
- Tagboard
- Markers
- Scissors
- String or yarn
- Hole punch
- Lamination paper

Dramatic Play

Directions

1. Cut four pieces of tagboard (see the accompanying photo).

2. Using markers, draw a girl's face on a piece of tagboard.

3. Print the word "Goldilocks" under the picture.

4. Using markers, draw a Papa Bear, a Mama Bear, and a Baby Bear on the three remaining pieces of tagboard.

5. Label each character.

6. Laminate all pieces.

7. Using a hole punch, create two holes in the top corners of each character piece.

8. Cut and tie a length of string or yarn to create a neckpiece for each character's card.

Teaching/Learning Strategies

- After reading the book *Goldilocks and the Three Bears,* allow the children to take turns being one of the characters and acting out the story. Include such story props as bowls, spoons, and chairs.

- Leave the props in the storytelling area for the children to retell stories.

- Consider preparing props for such stories as *The Three Little Pigs, Little Red Riding Hood, Jack and the Beanstalk,* and *Cinderella,* as well as other appropriate folk and fairy tales.

- When developmentally appropriate, provide materials for the children to create their own props.

Halloween Wooden Spoon Puppets

Developmental Goals

1. Develop oral language skills.
2. Develop expressive and receptive language skills.
3. Develop fine motor coordination skills.
4. Develop eye-hand coordination skills.
5. Practice retelling a story.

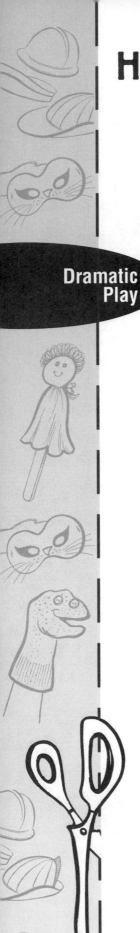

Dramatic Play

Related Curriculum Themes

Halloween   Communication
Puppets   Storytelling
Acting

Curriculum Areas

Language Arts
Social Studies

Preparation Tools and Materials

- Wooden spoons
- Fabric pieces
- Yarn
- Green tempera paint
- Markers
- Glue or hot glue gun

Directions

1. To make the ghost puppet, cover a wooden spoon with a 24" square of white fabric, tie a piece of yarn around the base of the spoon to secure the fabric to the spoon, and use a marker to draw eyes and mouth (see the accompanying photo).

2. To create the witch puppet, paint a wooden spoon with green tempera paint; let it dry; wrap a 20" black piece of fabric around the base of the spoon, securing it with a piece of yarn; glue black yarn pieces to the spoon to represent hair; glue a triangle-shaped piece of fabric to the spoon to resemble a hat; and use a marker to draw eyes, a nose, and a mouth (see the accompanying photo).

Teaching/Learning Strategies

- Use the spoon puppets to tell a group story, then set the puppets out in the story-telling area of the classroom, allowing the children to retell the story.

- When developmentally appropriate, give the children materials to create their own puppets.

Hamburger Box Puppets

Developmental Goals

1. Develop expressive language skills.
2. Experiment and discover new ways of using materials.
3. Develop small motor coordination skills.
4. Develop eye-hand coordination skills.
5. Practice expressing feelings.
6. Develop eye-hand coordination.

Related Curriculum Themes

Puppets   Storytelling
Communication   Feelings
Containers

Curriculum Areas

Language Arts
Social Studies

Preparation Tools and Materials

- One styrofoam hamburger box
- Contact paper
- Yarn
- Felt
- Glue
- Scissors
- Stapler
- Piece of elastic, 4" x 1"

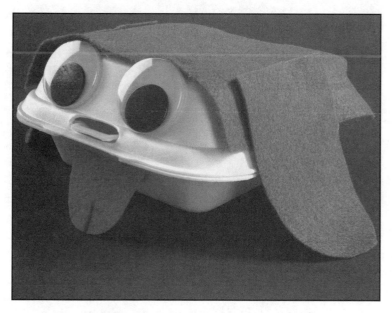

Directions

1. If the styrofoam box was a food container, disinfect it with bleach.
2. Cover the top portion of the styrofoam box with contact paper (see the accompanying photo).
3. Decorate the box with yarn and felt to represent a person or an animal.
4. Staple a piece of elastic to the outside crease or spine of the box to make a handle for manipulating the puppet.

Teaching/Learning Strategies

- Introduce the puppet at group time, then place the puppet in the storytelling area or the dramatic play area with a mirror and/or puppet stage. The children can use the puppets during self-directed play.

- Extend this activity for older children by giving them materials to make their own puppets.

Household Puppets

Developmental Goals

1. Develop expressive language skills.
2. Develop social skills.
3. Experiment and discover new ways of using materials.
4. Develop eye-hand coordination skills.
5. Practice expressing feelings.

Related Curriculum Themes

Puppets
Communication
Community Helpers

Families
Tools
Storytelling

Curriculum Areas

Language Arts
Art

Preparation Tools and Materials

- Household cleaning brushes (e.g., whisk brooms and scrub brushes)
- Fabric, felt, ribbon, and yarn scraps
- Plastic eyes (optional)
- Glue or hot glue gun
- Scissors
- Ball fringe

Directions

1. Using scraps of fabric, felt, ribbon, and yarn, make facial features and clothing for people or animals.

2. Glue the facial features, clothing, and plastic eyes onto the household brushes.

Teaching/Learning Strategies

- Introduce the puppets during group time, then encourage the children to use the puppets with a puppet theater made out of a cardboard box or a discarded television console with the glass removed.

- If developmentally appropriate, the children can decorate a large cardboard box for a puppet theater.

Nylon Mask Puppets

Developmental Goals

1. Develop expressive language skills.
2. Experiment and discover new ways of using materials.
3. Develop fine motor coordination.
4. Develop eye-hand coordination skills.
5. Practice expressing feelings.

Dramatic Play

Related Curriculum Themes

Puppets	Communication
Creativity	Feelings
Nursery Rhymes	Storytelling

Curriculum Areas

Language Arts
Social Studies

Preparation Tools and Materials

- Wire coat hangers
- Masking tape
- Nylon pantyhose
- Scissors
- Glue
- Material scraps
- Pipe cleaners

Directions

1. Bend the coat hanger to form a circle (see the accompanying photo).
2. Pull the nylon pantyhose tightly over the coat hanger form.
3. Wrap the nylon pantyhose around the coat hanger and secure it with masking tape.
4. Decorate the puppet with material and pipe cleaners to represent story characters, community helpers, or animals or other people.

Teaching/Learning Strategies

- Consider using these puppets to tell the story of *The Three Little Pigs*. Encourage the children to retell the story.

- When developmentally appropriate, the children can use the masks as puppets.

Paper Plate Meals

Developmental Goals

1. Identify different kinds of foods.
2. Identify foods eaten for breakfast, lunch, and dinner.
3. Develop problem-solving skills.
4. Develop visual discrimination skills.

Related Curriculum Themes

Foods   Home
School

Curriculum Areas

Social Studies
Health

Preparation Tools and Materials

- Paper plates
- Food pictures cut from magazines
- Scissors
- Construction paper (optional)
- Glue or glue stick
- Lamination paper

Directions

1. Cut food pictures from magazines. Look for varied items for breakfast, lunch, and dinner.

2. To make the pictures sturdy, use glue or a glue stick to attach the pictures to construction paper, then cut the pictures out.

3. Laminate the food pictures.

Teaching/Learning Strategies

- Place paper plates and food pictures in the small manipulatives or dramatic play area of the classroom. Encourage the children to first determine which foods go together to create an appealing meal, then to place the food pictures on paper plates.

Paper Plate Puppets

Developmental Goals

1. Develop listening and auditory memory skills.
2. View situations from others' perspectives.
3. Develop expressive and receptive language skills.
4. Develop social interaction skills.
5. Develop fine motor coordination skills.
6. Develop eye-hand coordination skills.

Dramatic Play

Related Curriculum Themes

Emotions	Friends
Happy/Sad	Community
Communication	Helpers
Puppets	People in
Toys	My World
Art	Storytelling
We Act	

Curriculum Areas

Language Arts
Social Studies

Preparation Tools and Materials

- Disposable plates, paper or plastic
- Glue
- Tongue depressor or craft stick
- Felt, fur, fabric, and yarn scraps
- Watercolor markers
- Stapler or glue
- Scissors

Directions

1. On the back of each paper plate, draw the face of a person or an animal.

2. Cut facial features from the felt pieces.

3. Glue the pieces onto the plate.

4. Insert a wooden tongue depressor or craft stick between the plates and glue them together.

Teaching/Learning Strategies

- These puppets, as well as others, can be used by one child or a group of children to act out stories.

- A puppet theater will enhance stimulation.

- You can extend the activity by letting the children design and make their own puppets.

Potholder Puppets

Developmental Goals

1. Develop expressive language skills.
2. Experiment and discover new ways of using materials.
3. Develop fine motor coordination skills.
4. Develop eye-hand coordination skills.
5. Practice expressing feelings.

Dramatic Play

Related Curriculum Themes

Animals   Storytelling
Puppets   Communication
Can Be Adapted to Any Theme

Curriculum Areas

Language Arts
Social Studies

Preparation Tools and Materials

- Potholders
- Felt and fabric scraps
- Plastic craft eyes
- Scissors
- Craft glue or hot glue gun
- Strips of 1" elastic
- Needle and thread
- Protective fabric spray (optional)

Directions

1. Decorate each potholder using the felt scraps and movable eyes (see the accompanying photo).

2. On the back of the potholder, glue or sew a 1" x 4" strip of elastic. (Sewing is usually more durable.)

3. If desired, spray the puppet with protective fabric spray to keep it clean and prevent spotting.

Teaching/Learning Strategies

- Show the children how to place the elastic strips over their hands to hold the puppets.

- Prepare potholder puppets to depict a favorite story, such as *The Three Little Pigs* or *Goldilocks and the Three Bears*.

- Adding a puppet stage or theater to the classroom environment can help promote the children's interest in puppets.

Table Place Settings

Developmental Goals

1. Visually discriminate.
2. Practice matching.
3. Develop problem-solving skills.
4. Develop eye-hand coordination skills.

Related Curriculum Themes

My Home   Manners
Foods   Shapes
Restaurant

Curriculum Area

Social Studies

Preparation Tools and Materials

- Four vinyl placemats
- Construction paper or solid-color contact paper
- Scissors
- Glue
- Set of dishes and silverware

Directions

1. Trace and cut from construction paper or solid-color contact paper four plates, glasses, forks, knives, and spoons.

2. Attach each place setting outline to a placemat (see the accompanying photo). Use glue when using construction paper.

Teaching/Learning Strategies

- Use the placemats in the dramatic play area with the matching dishes and silverware. Children can practice setting the table. Additional props to add to the area include a tablecloth, napkins, and a plastic vase of flowers.

Tablecloth Road Map

Developmental Goals

1. Develop eye-hand coordination skills.
2. Practice cooperating.
3. Identify areas on a road map.

Dramatic Play

Related Curriculum Themes

Cars   Occupations
Wheels   Vehicles
Friends

Curriculum Area

Social Studies

Preparation Tools and Materials

- One light-colored vinyl tablecloth
- Permanent markers

Directions

1. Using permanent markers, draw roads, trees, and a pond on the vinyl tablecloth.
2. Allow the design to dry before use.

Teaching/Learning Strategies

- Place the road map near the block area on the floor. Provide additional props, such as small toy cars and trucks, road signs, and people figures. Encourage the children to drive the toy cars on the roads.

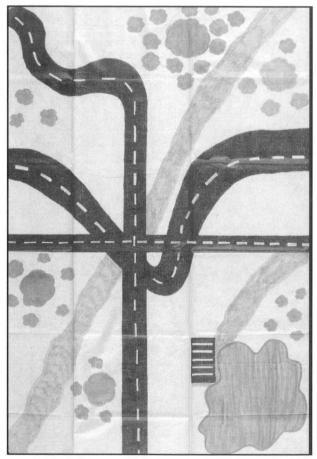

Traffic Light

Developmental Goals

1. Identify colors.
2. Develop language skills.
3. Develop shape identification.
4. Develop the concept of traffic signs.
5. Practice safety awareness.

Dramatic Play

Related Curriculum Themes

Signs   Shapes
Transportation   Safety
Colors   Communication

Curriculum Area

Social Studies

Preparation Tools and Materials

- One sheet of blue tagboard
- Acetate or cellophane paper (one sheet of red, one of yellow, and one of green)
- Masking tape
- Scissors
- Craft knife
- Lamination paper

Directions

1. Trace and cut from the tagboard the outline of a traffic light.

2. From the traffic light, cut three circles—one for each of the colored lights.

3. Cover the traffic light and pieces of acetate with lamination paper.

4. Using a craft knife, remove the lamination paper from the circles of the traffic light.

5. Using masking tape, attach the appropriate color acetate to the back of each circle.

Teaching/Learning Strategies

- Children learn safety rules through playful interaction with people and objects. Consequently, the traffic light should increase the children's awareness of their world. The adult should facilitate their involvement by pointing out the order of the colors and explaining the action each color represents. The adult may also wish to shine a flashlight behind the colors of the traffic light.

- This aid could also be used as a prop in the outdoor play area for trikes, scooters, and running games.

Games

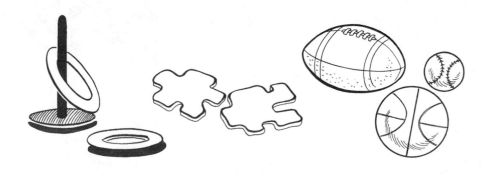

Bean Bag Hoop Toss

Developmental Goals

1. Develop gross motor skills.
2. Develop eye-hand coordination skills.
3. Develop prediction skills.
4. Develop problem-solving skills.
5. Practice the prosocial behavior of turn taking.

Related Curriculum Themes

Rainbows   Shapes
Color(s)   Games

Curriculum Areas

Physical Education
Math

Games

Preparation Tools and Materials

- Wire hangers or gold craft rings
- Bean bags
- Yarn
- Wire cutters
- Masking tape
- Scissors

Directions

1. Form circles (rings) using wire hangers.
2. Cut excess wire with wire cutters.
3. Wrap wire with masking tape to cover sharp edges.
4. Tie yarn at a starting point.
5. Begin wrapping yarn around the ring.
6. When complete, tie the yarn in a double knot.
7. Have the children toss or throw the bean bags through the hoops.

Teaching/Learning Strategies

- Place the hoops on the floor, hang them, or prop them against a wall.
- Observe the children's skill levels. If needed, move the hoops closer or farther away.

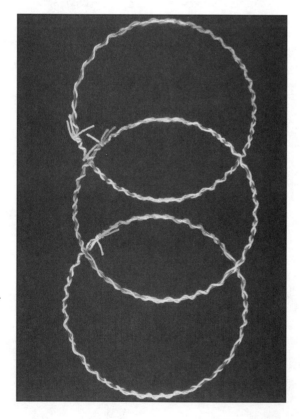

Bean Bag Toss

Developmental Goals

1. Develop eye-hand coordination skills.
2. Develop small muscle skills.
3. Develop the prosocial behavior of turn taking.
4. Encourage problem solving.
5. Practice predicting.

Related Curriculum Themes

Sports	Clowns
Animals	Boxes
Pets	Games
Shapes	

Curriculum Area

Large Muscle

Preparation Tools and Materials

- One piece of plywood, 30" x 36"
- Paint (different colors for each picture)
- Fabric for bags
- Filling for bags (beans, popcorn, rice, or sand)
- Needle and thread or sewing machine
- Paper
- Sandpaper
- Scissors

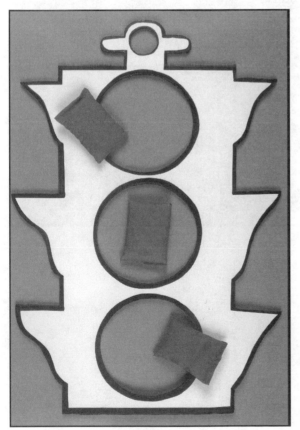

Directions

Frame

1. On a piece of 24" x 36" plywood or large, heavy, cardboard box, draw a picture related to your theme (see the accompanying photo).

2. Cut a hole. Hole size can vary.

Bags

1. Cut two pieces of fabric for each bean bag.

2. Sew the wrong sides of the fabric together, leaving an opening large enough to fill the bag.

3. Turn the bag right side out, and fill it with dried peas, beans, rice, sawdust, popcorn, or sand.

4. Sew the opening closed using a short stitch.

Teaching/Learning Strategies

- Depending on the developmental level of the children, vary the size of the hole on the frame. Young children need large holes.

- Using making tape, create a line on which the children should stand while tossing the bean bag. To make the game more challenging, move the line farther from the frame.

Dinosaur Footprints Game Board

Developmental Goals

1. Identify printed numerals.
2. Practice counting.
3. Develop problem-solving skills.
4. Develop cooperation skills.
5. Develop visual discrimination skills.

Related Curriculum Themes

Dinosaurs   Numbers
Games   Friends

Curriculum Areas

Math
Social Studies

Preparation Tools and Materials

- One sheet of tagboard
- Construction paper
- Dinosaur stickers or clip art
- Scissors
- Markers
- Glue or glue stick
- Lamination paper

Directions

1. Cut from construction paper a set of dinosaur footprints (see the accompanying photo).

2. Using glue or a glue stick, attach the dinosaur footprints to the tagboard in a curve-shaped line.

3. Use a marker to print the word "Start" on the first footprint.

4. Use a marker to print the words "Finish" and "Roll a 6 to win!" on the last footprint.

5. Randomly print the numerals 1 through 6 on the remaining footprint pieces.

6. Print the words "Dinosaur Footprints" on construction paper strips, and use glue to attach them to the game board.

7. Decorate the board with dinosaur stickers.

8. Laminate the game board.

Teaching/Learning Strategies

- Place the dinosaur footprints game board on a table or on the floor with game pieces, markers, and one die. To play the game, all the children choose game pieces and place them at the beginning of the path. The children take turns rolling the die and counting the dots on the top face of the die. They then move their game pieces along the path until reaching the first footprint with the corresponding numeral. The first child to roll a 6 at the last footprint wins. A 6 must be rolled to win.

Dog and Bones Folder Game

Developmental Goals

1. Develop the prosocial behavior of turn taking.
2. Visually discriminate.
3. Develop fine motor coordination skills.
4. Develop eye-hand coordination skills.
5. Practice following directions.
6. Practice counting.

Related Curriculum Themes

Animals	Bones
Pets	Puppies
Dogs	Games

Curriculum Areas

Math
Social Studies

Preparation Tools and Materials

- Colored file folder
- White and black construction paper
- Paper punch
- Felt-tip markers
- Glue or glue stick
- Scissors
- Lamination paper

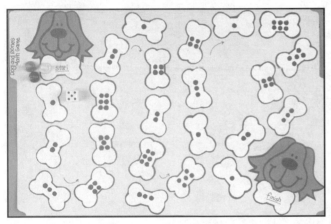

Directions

1. Cut and glue on the folder 2" white bones in a gameboard format (see the accompanying photo).

2. Using a paper punch, prepare small, black circles.

3. Glue the black circles onto the bones, with six being the highest number. The bones can be placed on the game board sequentially (e.g., 1–6) with the sequence repeated several times, or they can be placed randomly (e.g., 2, 6, 4, 3, 1, 5, 6, 2, 1, and so on).

4. Trace and cut from construction paper two dogs with bones in their mouths.

5. Decorate the dogs using watercolor markers.

6. Print the word "Start" on one dog and "Finish" on the other.

7. Glue the "Start" dog to the appropriate place on the folder.

8. Glue the "Finish" dog to the appropriate place on the folder.

9. Cut four round circles, to be used as board markers, from construction paper scraps.

10. Laminate the file folder game and marker pieces.

Teaching/Learning Strategies

- This game is best played in small groups or with a teacher and child.

- The game is played by shaking a die and moving a marker to the bone that corresponds to the number of circles on the die. The game ends when a marker lands next to or closest to the finish.

- For variation, a number, as opposed to the dots, can be placed on each dog bone.

Farmer in the Dell Game Pieces

Developmental Goals

1. Develop the prosocial behavior of turn taking.
2. Develop auditory memory skills.
3. Develop an appreciation of music.
4. Develop expressive language skills.

Related Curriculum Themes

Farms   Music
Occupations   Friends
Games

Curriculum Areas

Social Studies   Language Arts
Music

Preparation Tools and Materials

- One sheet of white tagboard
- Colored felt-tip markers
- Scissors
- Yarn
- Paper punch
- Lamination paper

Directions

1. On the tagboard sheet, draw the figures from "The Farmer in the Dell": a piece of cheese, a mouse, a cat, a dog, a nurse, a child, a farmer, and a spouse (see the accompanying photo).

2. Decorate the figures with felt-tip markers.

3. Cut out the pieces with scissors.

4. Laminate each piece.

5. Punch two holes near the top of each tagboard figure.

6. Cut a length of yarn that is long enough to fit over a child's head, string it through the holes, and tie.

Teaching/Learning Strategies

- Use the game pieces while playing "The Farmer in the Dell." As each character is introduced, choose a child and place the appropriate game piece over his or her head. After the group game, put the game pieces in the dramatic play area of the classroom for use during self-directed play periods.

Games

54

Goblin in the Dark Game Pieces

Developmental Goals

1. Practice following directions.
2. Develop the prosocial behavior of turn taking.
3. Develop expressive language skills.
4. Learn traditional Halloween symbols.

Related Curriculum Themes

Halloween   Friends
Games   Make Believe

Curriculum Areas

Social Studies
Language Arts

Preparation Tools and Materials

- One piece of orange tagboard, 8½" x 9"
- One piece of black tagboard, 8" x 7"
- One piece of black tagboard, 8½" x 6"
- One piece of white tagboard, 6" x 10"
- One piece of white tagboard, 8½" x 11"
- One piece of green tagboard, 7" x 10"
- Colored construction paper
- Yarn
- Colored markers
- Scissors
- Glue or glue stick
- Paper punch
- Lamination paper

Games

Directions

1. From the tagboard, trace and cut a figure representing an orange pumpkin, a black bat, a black cat, a white ghost, a witch, and a goblin.
2. Decorate each figure, adding details with felt-tip markers and construction paper (see the accompanying photo).
3. Laminate all pieces.
4. Punch two holes near the top of each tagboard figure.
5. Cut a length of yarn that is long enough to fit over a child's head, string it through the holes, and tie.

Teaching/Learning Strategies

- This game can be played to the following tune and directions of "The Farmer in the Dell,":

  THE GOBLIN IN THE DARK
  1. The goblin in the dark,
     The goblin in the dark,
     Hi, ho on Halloween,
     The goblin in the dark.
  2. The goblin takes a witch . . .
  3. The witch takes a cat . . .
  4. The cat takes a bat . . .
  5. The bat takes a ghost . . .
  6. The ghost takes a pumpkin . . .
  7. The pumpkin stands alone,
     The pumpkin stands alone,
     Hi, ho on Halloween,
     The pumpkin stands alone.

Continue singing the verses until each child has represented a figure. Place the game pieces in an area of the classroom for use during self-directed play periods.

Halloween and Ghost Folder Game

Developmental Goals

1. Develop the prosocial behavior of turn taking.
2. Develop visual discrimination skills.
3. Develop fine motor coordination skills.
4. Practice following directions.
5. Practice counting.

Related Curriculum Themes

Halloween   Games
Numbers

Curriculum Areas

Math   Language Arts
Social Studies

Preparation Tools and Materials

- Orange file folder
- White construction paper
- Orange construction paper scraps

- Colored markers
- Glue or glue stick
- Paper punch
- Scissors
- Lamination paper

Directions

1. Draw and cut approximately 30 small ghost shapes, ½" x 1", from white construction paper (see the accompanying photo).

2. Using a paper punch, make small, orange circles.

3. Glue the circles onto the ghosts, six being the highest number.

4. Glue the ghosts to an open file folder sequentially (e.g., 1–6, repeated several times) or randomly (2, 5, 3, 4, 6, 1, 3, 4, 6 and so on).

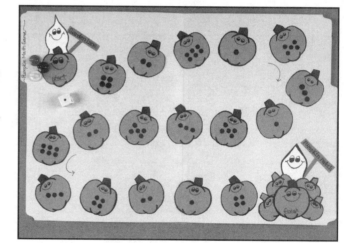

5. With a marker, print "Start" and "Finish" on separate ghost pieces.

6. Glue each piece in the appropriate place on the folder.

7. Cut four round circles, to be used as board markers, from construction paper scraps.

8. Laminate all the pieces.

Teaching/Learning Strategies

- Provide a die and give each player a marker. Let the children take turns rolling the die and moving their markers to the nearest ghost with the corresponding set of dots. The game ends when a marker lands next to or closest to the finish.

- For older children, extend this activity by making a spinner with numbers.

Heart Bingo Game

Developmental Goals

1. Develop listening skills.
2. Identify printed letters.
3. Identify printed numerals.
4. Develop the prosocial behavior of turn taking.

Related Curriculum Themes

Valentine's Day   Red
Games   Letters
Numbers   Friends

Curriculum Areas

Language Arts   Math
Social Studies

Preparation Tools and Materials

- Construction paper or tagboard
- Permanent markers
- Scissors (craft scissors optional)
- Ruler
- Circles to cover numbers
- Lamination paper

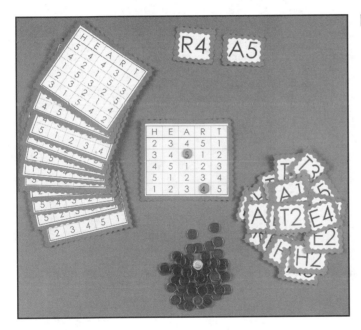

Directions

1. Prepare bingo grid cards for each player (see the accompanying photo).

   a. Cut construction paper or tagboard into 9" x 7½" pieces.

   b. Use a ruler and marker to divide each card vertically into five equal sections.

   c. Use a ruler and marker to divide each card horizontally into six equal sections.

   d. Print the letters of the word "Heart" across the top grid sections of each card.

   e. Randomly fill in the rest of the cards with numerals 1 through 5.

2. Prepare bingo calling cards (see the accompanying photo).

   a. Cut construction paper or tagboard into 3" x 3" squares.

   b. Print a letter and numeral on each card to correspond to a grid on each player card.

3. Laminate all game pieces.

Teaching/Learning Strategies

- The bingo cards can be adapted to any curriculum theme.

- Depending on the developmental level of the children, the bingo grid cards can be designed with more or fewer spaces. Similarly, the numerals selected for the bingo cards can vary depending on the children's abilities.

Sticker Dominoes

Developmental Goals

1. Develop visual discrimination skills.
2. Develop eye-hand coordination skills.
3. Practice following directions.
4. Develop the prosocial behavior of turn taking.
5. Develop problem-solving skills.

Related Curriculum Themes

Games   Symbols
Friends
Can Be Adapted to Any Theme

Curriculum Areas

Language Arts   Social Studies
Math

Preparation Tools and Materials

- One large piece colored tagboard
- Four different sets of four stickers
- Scissors
- Back felt-tip marker
- Lamination paper

Directions

1. Cut the tagboard into 32 pieces, 6" x 3".
2. With a marker, divide each tagboard piece in half to create two equal squares.
3. Place one sticker on each half of the tagboard.
4. Like dominoes, mix the sticker combinations on each tagboard piece.
5. Laminate all pieces.

Teaching/Learning Strategies

- Place this activity in the game center or on a table in the small motor area for use during self-directed play. The object of this activity is to match stickers (see the accompanying photo).

- Some children may need to be guided by an adult to see possible solutions.

Sticker Lotto Game

Developmental Goals

1. Develop visual discrimination skills.
2. Develop eye-hand coordination skills.
3. Develop small muscle coordination skills.
4. Develop the prosocial behavior of turn taking.

Related Curriculum Themes

Animals	Fruits
Zoo	Vegetables
Farm	Colors
Dogs	Shapes
Bugs	Numerals
Birds	Alphabet letters

Curriculum Areas

Math	Social Studies
Language Arts	

Preparation Tools and Materials

- Four pieces of tagboard, 8" x 12"
- Twenty-four tagboard cards, 4" x 4"
- Watercolor markers
- Stickers of familiar objects or clip art
- Ruler
- Lamination paper

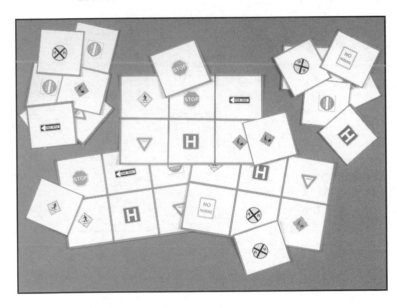

Directions

1. Using a watercolor marker, create six spaces of equal size by dividing the four tagboard pieces in thirds vertically and in half horizontally.

2. Paste a sticker, use clip art, or draw a symbol on each of the 24 cards and on each space on the game board (see the accompanying photo).

3. Laminate all lotto game pieces.

Teaching/Learning Strategies

- To be developmentally appropriate for younger children, design the boards with only three spaces as opposed
  to six. The children can then place the matching number below the card, allowing them to recognize when one space or all spaces are filled.

- The objects should be varied to represent the children's interest or a curriculum theme.

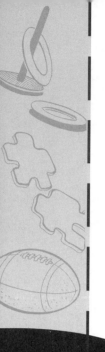

Sticker Tracing Mazes

Developmental Goals

1. Develop visual discrimination skills.
2. Develop eye-hand coordination skills.
3. Develop small muscle coordination skills.
4. Develop the prosocial behavior of turn taking.
5. Practice problem solving.

Related Curriculum Themes

Writing   Paper
Writing tools
Can Be Adapted to Any Theme

Curriculum Area

Language Arts

Games

Preparation Tools and Materials

- Six pieces of card stock, 11" x 9"
- Stickers or hand-drawn symbols
- Black marker
- Glue
- Lamination paper

Directions

1. Attach a row of stickers to the left-hand side of a piece of card stock (see the accompanying photo).

2. Attach identical stickers to the right-hand side of the card stock in a different sequence.

3. Using the photograph as a guide, draw varying lines from one symbol to another.

4. Laminate each card.

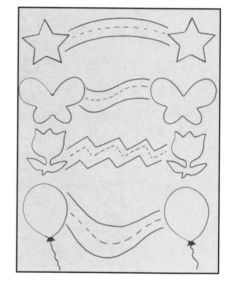

Teaching/Learning Strategies

- This activity can be placed in the writing center. Display the cards and provide watercolor markers. Encourage the children to trace on or between the lines connecting the symbols. Clean the cards by wiping with a damp cloth or paper towel.

Summer Fun Lacing Cards

Developmental Goals

1. Develop small muscle coordination skills.
2. Develop eye-hand coordination skills.
3. Practice problem solving.

Related Curriculum Themes

Summer   Colors
Friends   Games
Shapes

Curriculum Areas

Language Arts
Science

Preparation Tools and Materials

- Six pieces of 11" x 14" tagboard or colored card stock
- Markers
- Hole punch
- Lamination paper
- Long, thick shoelaces

Directions

1. Draw and cut from varied colors of tagboard such symbols of summer as a football, butterfly, kite, strawberry, sun, people, shorts, and a pail.
2. Use a marker to add details and to print the name of each item.
3. Laminate all pieces.
4. Use a hole punch to create a series of holes around the edges of all pieces.

Teaching/Learning Strategies

- Place the cards on a table in the classroom. Provide such lacing materials as a sturdy string, shoelace, or piece of yarn. Tie one end of the lacing material to each card. This will prevent the lacing materials from being misplaced.

Transportation Tracing Cards

Developmental Goals

1. Identify basic shapes.
2. Develop eye-hand coordination skills.
3. Associate printed words with their symbols.
4. Practice forming letters.

Related Curriculum Themes

Letters	Our World
Communication	Shapes
Words	Writing

Curriculum Areas

Language Arts
Social Studies

Games

Preparation Tools and Materials

- Nine pieces of card stock, 8½" x 11"
- Markers
- Scissors
- Lamination paper

Directions

1. Draw and cut transportation shapes from the card stock pieces. Examples include a car, train, truck, bus, boat, bike, foot, airplane, and skate.

2. Use markers to add detail to the transportation cards.

3. Use a marker to print, in dotted outline letter formation, the name of the object on each card (see the accompanying photo).

4. Laminate all pieces.

Teaching/Learning Strategies

- Give the children watercolor markers or a grease pencil to trace the alphabet letters. Also give the children a damp sponge or a spray bottle of water and paper towel to remove their markings.

Umbrella Game Board

Developmental Goals

1. Identify printed words.
2. Practice counting.
3. Develop problem-solving skills.
4. Develop cooperation skills.
5. Develop visual discrimination skills.
6. Develop eye-hand coordination skills.

Related Curriculum Themes

Rain	Friends
Spring	Numbers
Water	Games

Curriculum Areas

Math
Social Studies

Preparation Tools and Materials

- One sheet of light-blue tagboard
- Construction paper
- Die-cut umbrella shapes (optional)
- Markers
- Scissors
- Glue or glue stick
- White or yellow paint (optional)
- Lamination paper

Games

Directions

1. Cut from construction paper a set of umbrella shapes, or use die-cut shapes (see the accompanying photo).

2. Using glue or a glue stick, attach the umbrella shapes to the tagboard in a curved line.

3. Use a marker to print the word "Start" on the first umbrella shape.

4. Use a marker to print the word "Finish" and the numeral 6 on the last shape.

5. Randomly, print the numerals 1 through 6 on the remaining umbrella pieces. (Optional: Print the words "Roll again" under a few of the numerals.)

6. To add interest, draw and cut from construction paper a small duck and a larger umbrella shape.

(continues)

Umbrella Game Board

(continued)

7. Type or use a marker to print the following verse on the larger umbrella:

SO MANY UMBRELLAS
Umbrellas can be red,
Umbrellas can be blue.
Umbrellas can be patterned,
With lots of colors, too!

8. Use glue to attach the duck and larger umbrella shape to a corner of the tagboard.

9. If desired, use white or yellow paint to create raindrop shapes on the tagboard.

10. Laminate the game board.

Teaching/Learning Strategies

- Place the umbrella game board on a table or on the floor with game pieces and markers and one die. To play the game, all players choose a game piece and place it at the umbrella labeled "Start." Each player in turn rolls the die and counts the number of dots on the top face of the die. The player then moves his or her game piece along the path until reaching the first umbrella shape with the corresponding numeral. If a player lands on an umbrella labeled "Roll again," he or she immediately takes another turn. The first player to roll a 6 at the last umbrella is the winner.

Games

Valentine Puzzles

Developmental Goals

1. Develop visual discrimination skills.
2. Develop problem-solving skills.
3. Develop eye-hand coordination skills.
4. Develop small muscle coordination skills.

Related Curriculum Themes

Valentine's Day   Paper
Friendship   Puzzles

Curriculum Areas

Language Arts
Social Studies

Preparation Tools and Materials

- Red or pink card stock pieces, 4½" x 6"
- Valentine cards
- Glue or glue stick
- Scissors
- Lamination paper

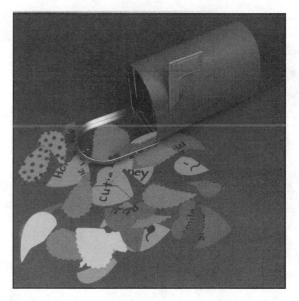

Directions

1. Glue a Valentine card onto each card stock piece.

2. Cut each puzzle in half, horizontally or vertically, creating varied cutting patterns—zigzag, wavy, or straight edge. The complexity of the cutting patterns should suit the developmental level of the children.

3. Laminate all puzzle pieces.

Teaching/Learning Strategies

- To promote learning as an interactive process, place the puzzle pieces on a table or on the floor for use during self-directed play periods. If needed, encourage the children to locate the matching halves of the puzzles. Children may elect to participate individually or in small groups.

- This learning activity could be adapted for other holidays, including Easter, Halloween, Thanksgiving, St. Patrick's Day, Christmas, and Hanukkah.

Wallpaper Puzzles

Developmental Goals

1. Develop visual discrimination skills.
2. Develop eye-hand coordination skills.
3. Promote small motor skills.
4. Review color concepts.

Related Curriculum Themes

Easter	Colors
Shapes	Puzzles
Paper	Games
Designs	

Curriculum Areas

Language Arts
Social Studies

Preparation Tools and Materials

- Wallpaper scraps
- Scissors
- Lamination paper

Games

Directions

1. Cut shapes, such as ovals and stars, from wallpaper scraps.

2. Using varied creative patterns—zigzag, wavy, straight edge—cut the shapes in half. The complexity of the cutting patterns should suit the developmental needs of the children.

3. Laminate the puzzle pieces.

Teaching/Learning Strategies

- Place wallpaper puzzles on a table or on the floor. Encourage the children to complete the puzzles.

- For children who cannot fit the puzzle pieces together, the adult acts as facilitator, providing clues and suggestions. Once mastered, the children may initiate and repeat the process.

Watermelon Game

Developmental Goals
1. Develop visual discrimination skills.
2. Develop eye-hand coordination skills.
3. Develop small muscle coordination skills.
4. Recognize alphabet letters.

Related Curriculum Themes
Letters	Summer
Nutrition	Fruit
Seeds	Writing
Communication	Colors
Foods	

Curriculum Areas
Social Studies
Language Arts

Preparation Tools and Materials
- Pink tagboard
- Construction paper
- Manuscript or writing paper
- Green and black markers
- Scissors
- Glue, glue stick, or hot glue gun
- Lamination paper

Games

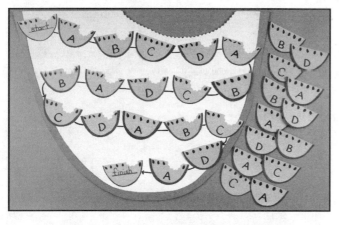

Directions
1. Draw half a watermelon on a pink piece of tagboard (see the accompanying photo).
2. Cut out the watermelon shape.
3. Draw the watermelon rind, and color the area green using a marker.
4. Outline the edges of the rind with a black marker.
5. Construct two sets of small watermelon slices from colored construction paper.
6. Add detail by outlining with a green marker.
7. Print the word "Start" on one watermelon slice and "Finish" on another.
8. On the remaining slices, print uppercase alphabet letters.
9. Repeat on the second set of watermelon slices.
10. Glue or paste the first set of letters on the watermelon.
11. Use a green marker to draw a line from one melon to another, creating a game board pattern.
12. Laminate the board and pieces.

Teaching/Learning Strategies
- First, place the game board and pieces upside down on a table. Instruct the children to take turns drawing pieces and placing them on the board. The board can also be used by one child to match the letters.
- The game can be adapted. For example, the background shape could be a food such as a squash, cantaloupe, or strawberry. This activity also could be adapted for holidays. Examples include a pumpkin for Halloween, a turkey for Thanksgiving, rabbits or eggs for Easter, and hearts for Valentine's Day.

Zoo Lotto Game

Developmental Goals

1. Develop visual discrimination skills.
2. Develop eye-hand coordination skills.
3. Develop the prosocial behavior of turn taking.
4. Develop small muscle coordination skills.
5. Practice following directions.

Related Curriculum Themes

Zoo   Animals
Occupations   Games

Curriculum Areas

Social Studies
Language Arts

Preparation Tools and Materials

- Four sheets of tagboard, 5" x 8"
- Sixteen pieces of tagboard, 2½" x 2½"
- Black felt-tip marker
- Scissors
- Ruler
- Zoo stickers, die cuts, clip art, or wrapping paper shapes
- Lamination paper

Directions

1. With the marker, divide each tagboard piece in half vertically and in half horizontally to create four spaces of equal size, 2½" x 2½" (see the accompanying photo).

2. Cut the remaining space on the tagboard piece to represent an entrance to a zoo.

3. Print the word "Zoo" at the top of each piece.

4. Glue different pictures onto each space on the game boards, and glue the matching pieces onto the 16 tagboard cards.

5. Laminate all pieces.

Teaching/Learning Strategies

- This activity can be played in groups of two to four children or one child and one adult. Give each child a game board. Place all player cards face down or in a pile. The children take turns drawing one card at a time and matching it to a space on his or her game board. When one player has filled all the spaces on his or her game board, turn the cards face down and begin again.

- Adapt the game to other themes. Holiday symbols can be used.

Games

Language Arts

Alphabet Letter Cards

Developmental Goals

1. Develop tactile awareness.
2. Recognize letters.
3. Visually discriminate.
4. Identify uppercase and lowercase letters.

Related Curriculum Themes

Shapes   Letters
Textures   Writing Tools

Curriculum Area

Language Arts

Preparation Tools and Materials

- Pieces of tagboard, 8" x 6"
- Scissors (craft scissors optional)
- Glue or glue stick

Directions

1. Squeeze glue onto tagboard pieces in the form of letters or shapes (see the accompanying photo).

2. Allow the glue to dry thoroughly.

Teaching/Learning Strategies

- Place the rubbings on a table in the writing or small motor center. Provide paper and large crayons. (For young children, remove the paper wrapper from the crayons.) If necessary, demonstrate the process of placing a thin piece of paper over the dried glue shapes. Then, rub a crayon over the forms to reveal the letters or shapes. Older children may be able to create their own alphabet letter cards.

- To vary this activity, make a set of numeral or shape cards by following the same procedures.

Language
Arts

Alphabet Match

Developmental Goals

1. Develop visual discrimination skills.
2. Develop problem-solving skills.
3. Identify alphabet letters.
4. Match upper- and lowercase alphabet letters.
5. Develop eye-hand coordination skills.
6. Develop small muscle coordination skills.

Related Curriculum Themes

Alphabet Letters   Communicating
Storytelling   Our World
Matching

Curriculum Area

Language Arts

Preparation Tools and Materials

- Six tagboard sheets, 10" x 12"
- Black watercolor marker
- Scissors
- Ruler
- Lamination paper

Directions

1. Cut a piece of tagboard into six 10"x 12" sections (the accompanying photo depicts one game board).

2. Use a marker to divide the 10" x 12" pieces of tagboard into 2" squares.

3. From tagboard, cut 104 cards, 2" x 2".

4. Print an uppercase alphabet letter in each of the 104 squares. Alphabet letters may be duplicated.

5. Print a lowercase and an uppercase alphabet letter on the large game board cards.

6. Laminate all pieces.

Teaching/Learning Strategies

- The children select one card at a time and check the large card until they locate the matching lowercase letter. They then place the card directly on top of its matching letter.

- This activity can be made self-correcting by printing the matching lowercase letter on the back of each cardboard square.

71

Alphabet Soup Match

Developmental Goals

1. Develop visual discrimination skills.
2. Develop problem-solving skills.
3. Develop the prosocial behavior of turn taking.
4. Learn alphabet letters.
5. Practice sequencing alphabet letters.
6. Develop eye-hand coordination skills.

Related Curriculum Themes

Alphabet Letters   Communication
Shapes   Writing
Names   Symbols
Print   Reading
Matching

Curriculum Area

Language Arts

Preparation Tools and Materials

- Four pieces of tagboard, 12" x 12"
- Twenty-six tagboard pieces, 1" square
- Watercolor marker
- Scissors
- Lamination paper

Language Arts

Directions

1. Cut the 12" x 12" tagboard pieces to resemble bowls. Use markers to add details.

2. Draw 26 squares for the alphabet letters on each bowl-shaped tagboard piece (see the accompanying photo).

3. Print some alphabet letters in the squares, but make sure some letters are missing on each card.

4. Print the missing alphabet letters on the tagboard squares.

5. Laminate all pieces.

Teaching/Learning Strategies

- Place the cards on a table in the writing or small manipulative area. This activity can be undertaken by an individual child or by small groups.

- A group of children can play this game by taking turns selecting a letter from the can. After identifying the letter, it should be placed on the correct position on the card. Some children may need help determining correct board placement.

- This chart could be made with uppercase letters or numerals. Moreover, the shape of the board could be adapted to numerous curriculum themes.

Chubby Little Snowman

Developmental Goals

1. Develop an appreciation for poetry.
2. Develop an appreciation for the printed word.
3. Experience a print-rich environment.
4. Develop visual discrimination skills.
5. Develop auditory discrimination skills.
6. Associate printed words with spoken words.

Related Curriculum Themes

Winter   Communication
Symbols   Rhymes and Poetry
Letters

Curriculum Area

Language Arts

Preparation Tools and Materials

- Tagboard
- Construction paper or sentence strips
- Colored markers
- Glue or glue stick
- Scissors (craft scissors optional)
- Lamination paper

Directions

1. Using a marker on construction paper or sentence strips, print the words and draw the illustrations for the following poem, "A Chubby Little Snowman":

   A CHUBBY LITTLE SNOWMAN
   A chubby little snowman had a carrot nose.
   Along came a bunny, and what do you suppose?
   That hungry little bunny, looking for his lunch,
   Ate the snowman's carrot nose. Nibble, nibble, crunch.

2. Use glue or a glue stick to attach the title and poem strips to the tagboard.
3. Add detail to the chart as desired.
4. Laminate the chart.

Teaching/Learning Strategies

- Introduce the poem "A Chubby Little Snowman" with the chart during group time. Encourage the children to recite the poem with you, then display the chart in the writing or language arts center. Give the children paper, crayons, pencils, and markers to illustrate the poem.

Clothespin Letters and Words

Developmental Goals

1. Match upper- and lowercase letters.
2. Observe printed words.
3. Develop small muscle coordination skills.
4. Develop visual discrimination skills.
5. Develop eye-hand coordination skills.

Related Curriculum Themes

Communication   Letters
Clothing   Words

Curriculum Area

Language Arts

Preparation Tools and Materials

- Rulers
- Wooden spring clothespins
- Index cards, construction paper, or tagboard
- Felt-tip permanent markers
- Scissors
- Lamination paper

Directions

1. Type or print a set of lowercase word cards on index cards, construction paper, or tagboard (see the accompanying photo).

2. Use a permanent felt-tip marker to print a set of uppercase letters on wooden clothespins.

3. Clip the clothespins on rulers for storage.

4. Laminate the word cards.

Teaching/Learning Strategies

- Place the cards and clothespins on a table. Demonstrate how to select a card, find a clothespin with an uppercase letter that matches each lowercase letter in the word, and detach the matching card to the original card. Then encourage the children to repeat this process.

- The word cards can be adapted to any curriculum theme. To make this activity more challenging, a set of lowercase letters can be printed on clothespins. Moreover, an extension of the activity would be to provide rulers or yardsticks. The children could place the clothespins on them in alphabetical order.

Cookie Sheet Magnet Board

Developmental Goals

1. Develop an appreciation of storytelling.
2. Develop auditory memory skills.
3. Develop sequencing skills.
4. Develop an understanding of order.
5. Practice retelling a story.

Related Curriculum Themes
Storytelling
Adaptable to Any Theme
(or Fingerplay)

Curriculum Areas
Language Arts   Math
Music

Preparation Tools and Materials
- Pizza pan or cookie sheet
- Cards, wrapping paper, or stickers
- Craft magnets or magnetic strips
- Spray paint (optional)
- Lamination paper

Directions

1. Decorate the background of the pizza pan or cookie sheet using spray paint, stickers, or other media.

2. Cut out pictures from cards or wrapping paper or use large stickers.

3. Place magnets on the backs of characters or pictures.

Language Arts

Teaching/Learning Strategies

- Use this teaching aid for telling a story, singing a song, or introducing a fingerplay. If needed, the words can be pasted to the backside. After using, place in a classroom area where the children can use this to retell the story, conduct fingerplay, or sing a song.

Feely Boxes

Developmental Goals

1. Develop tactile discrimination skills.
2. Practice predicting.
3. Develop small muscle coordination skills.
4. Develop eye-hand coordination skills.

Related Curriculum Themes

Touch   My World
Senses   Hands

Curriculum Areas

Science
Language Arts

Preparation Tools and Materials

- One pint-size plastic container (e.g., freezer food container or empty yogurt or cottage cheese container)
- One adult-size tube sock

Language Arts

Directions

1. Insert the plastic container all the way to the bottom of the sock.

2. Place items in the box: cotton balls, a clothespin, a crayon, a rock, a small block, a toy, and a coin.

Teaching/Learning Strategies

- Gather several small items to place in the feely box. To use, the children insert their hands into the sock and attempt to identify the objects by touch. The items can then be pulled out of the feely boxes to verify guesses.

- This game can be used again, and made more challenging, by changing the items in the boxes.

Find the Colors Chart

Developmental Goals

1. Develop visual discrimination skills.
2. Recognize that the spoken word can be represented in print.
3. Identify color words.
4. Develop eye-hand coordination skills.

Related Curriculum Themes
Colors
Art
Brushes

Curriculum Areas
Language Arts
Science
Art

Preparation Tools and Materials

- One sheet of white tagboard
- Red, orange, yellow, green, blue, and purple construction paper
- Scissors
- Markers
- Glue or glue stick
- Index cards, sentence strips, or construction paper
- Lamination paper

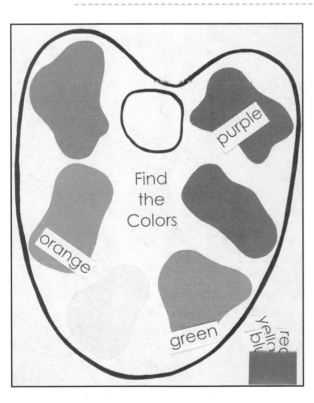

Directions

1. Use a marker to draw a large paint pallet shape on the tagboard (see the accompanying photo).

2. Cut irregular, rounded shapes from the construction paper to represent paint spots.

3. Using glue or a glue stick, attach the construction paper paint shapes to the tagboard.

4. Type or use a marker to print the title "Find the Colors" in the middle of the paint pallet shape.

5. Glue a construction paper rectangle to a bottom corner of the tagboard to create a pocket.

6. Type or use a marker to print color words on index cards, sentence strips, or construction paper.

7. Laminate all pieces and the chart.

Language Arts

Teaching/Learning Strategies

- Introduce the chart in a large group setting. If needed, demonstrate how to use the materials.

- To vary the activity, objects or pictures of different colors could be used. The activity can then be placed in an area of the classroom for the children's use.

Humpty Dumpty Chart

Developmental Goals

1. Develop an appreciation for the printed word.
2. Identify rhyming words.
3. Develop problem-solving skills.
4. Develop oral language skills.
5. Recognize that the spoken word can be represented in print.
6. Develop left-to-right progression skills.

Related Curriculum Themes
Nursery Rhymes
Eggs

Curriculum Area
Language Arts

Preparation Tools and Materials
- Red tagboard
- Construction paper or sentence strips
- Markers
- Glue, glue stick, or hot glue gun
- Scissors (craft scissors optional)
- Star stickers
- Lamination paper

Language Arts

Directions

1. Type or use a marker to print the following words of the Humpty Dumpty rhyme on construction paper or sentence strips:

   HUMPTY DUMPTY
   Humpty Dumpty sat on a wall,
   Humpty Dumpty had a great fall.
   All the king's horses and all the king's men,
   Couldn't put Humpty together again!

2. Use glue to attach the rhyme words to the lower right area of the red sheet of tagboard.

3. Draw and cut from construction paper a series of Humpty Dumpty figures during three stages of the rhyme. Include a broken egg figure (see the accompanying photo).

4. Use glue to attach the Humpty Dumpty figures in order on the tagboard.

5. Attach star stickers near the broken Humpty Dumpty figure.

6. Laminate the chart.

Teaching/Learning Strategies

- Introduce the Humpty Dumpty rhyme chart to the children during large group time. Point to the words as the children recite the rhyme. Allow the children to use the chart during self-selection time.

Marker Maze Cards

Developmental Goals

1. Develop small muscle coordination skills.
2. Develop eye-hand coordination skills.
3. Explore with writing tools.
4. Develop visual discrimination skills.

Related Curriculum Themes
Colors
Shapes

Curriculum Area
Language Arts

Preparation Tools and Materials
- Various colors of tagboard or construction paper
- Markers
- Scissors
- Lamination paper

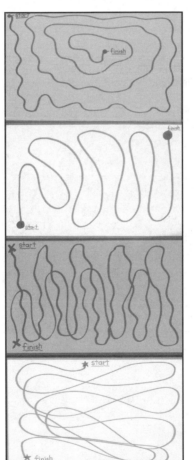

Directions

1. Cut tagboard or construction paper into 9″ x 12″ pieces.

2. On each piece, use a marker to draw an abstract design that has a starting and ending point (see the accompanying photo).

3. Mark the starting and ending points with a small star or circle shape.

4. Print the words "Start" and "Finish" on each card.

5. Laminate all pieces.

Language Arts

Teaching/Learning Strategies

- After introducing the cards in a large group setting, place them in the writing center or small manipulatives area of the classroom. Provide watercolor markers and a damp cloth or sponge. Encourage the children to start at the beginning of the design and trace over the marks on each card.

- Easier mazes could be used initially, with more difficult designs introduced as children become ready.

Object-Word Puzzles

Developmental Goals

1. Recognize lowercase letters.
2. Practice problem solving.
3. Develop visual discrimination skills.
4. Develop eye-hand coordination skills.
5. Associate the printed word with the symbol.
6. Develop an appreciation for the printed word.

Related Curriculum Themes

Puzzles	Shapes
Writing	Alphabet Letters
Communication	Matching
Our World	Words
Games	Symbols

Curriculum Area

Language Arts

Preparation Tools and Materials

- Fourteen pieces of colored tagboard, 6" x 9"
- Stickers, clip art, or photographs

- Glue or glue stick
- Watercolor markers
- Scissors
- Ruler
- Lamination paper

Language Arts

Directions

1. Glue stickers, clip art, or photographs to the upper half of the tagboard card.
2. Print the name of the object on the lower half of the card.
3. Laminate the pieces.
4. Cut the tagboard pieces in half, separating the pictures from the words (see the accompanying photo).

Teaching/Learning Strategies

- Place the teaching materials on a table. Demonstrate how to match the word to the object. To make this a self-correcting activity, print the name of the animal on the front or back of each card.

- The puzzle could also be constructed by using symbols related to other curriculum themes.

Picture Frame Felt Board

Developmental Goals

1. Develop an appreciation of storytelling.
2. Develop visual memory skills.
3. Develop auditory memory skills.
4. Develop receptive and expressive language skills.

Related Curriculum Themes
Storytelling
Adaptable to Any Theme

Curriculum Areas
Language Arts
Music

Preparation Tools and Materials
- Picture frame
- Sticky-back felt (or) felt with spray-mount adhesive

Directions

1. Carefully remove the glass from the picture frame.
2. Place the sticky-back felt onto cardboard backing, or affix the spray mount onto the cardboard and place the felt on cardboard backing.
3. Cut out excess felt.
4. Place the cardboard backing into proper position inside the frame.
5. Seal the frame.

Teaching/Learning Strategies

- Use the picture-frame felt board during storytelling. After telling the story, encourage the children to retell the story. To help the children, use a marker to print sequential numerals on the felt pieces.

Language Arts

Rainbow Chain Chart

Developmental Goals

1. Develop visual discrimination skills.
2. Develop color recognition skills.
3. Develop sequencing skills.
4. Develop eye-hand coordination skills.
5. Develop small motor coordination skills.

Related Curriculum Themes

Colors	Rainbows
Patterns	Holidays
Seasons	Paper

Curriculum Areas

Math	Social Studies
Language Arts	

Preparation Tools and Materials

- One sheet of tagboard, 22" x 28"
- Lamination paper
- Colored felt-tip markers

Language Arts

Directions

1. On a sheet of tagboard, use the markers to print the following instructions and draw the corresponding illustrations (see the accompanying photo).

   ### MAKE A RAINBOW CHAIN
   a. Illustrate the red chain.
   b. Illustrate the red and orange chain.
   c. Illustrate the red, orange, and yellow chain.
   d. Illustrate the red, orange, yellow, and green chain.
   e. Illustrate the red, orange, yellow, green, and blue chain.
   f. Illustrate the red, orange, yellow, green, blue, and purple chain.

2. Laminate the chart.

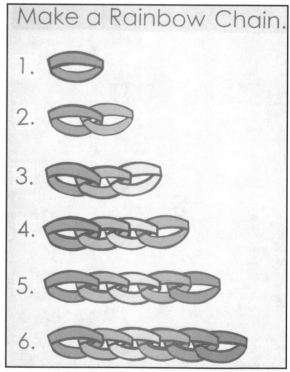

Make a Rainbow Chain.
1.
2.
3.
4.
5.
6.

Teaching/Learning Strategies

- Gather the materials needed to make the rainbow chains. For variety, adapt the chains to seasonal or holiday colors. In the fall, use red, orange, brown, and yellow. For Christmas, use red and white.

- Use the chains to decorate a bulletin board, a classroom door, children's lockers, or a room area.

Sandpaper Letter Match

Developmental Goals

1. Develop visual discrimination skills.
2. Develop eye-hand coordination skills.
3. Identify uppercase letters.
4. Identify lowercase letters.
5. Practice problem solving.

Related Curriculum Themes

Alphabet Letters   Communication
Words   Touch
Sounds   Letters in Our World
Shapes   Symbols

Curriculum Area

Language Arts

Preparation Tools and Materials

- Twenty pieces of tagboard
- Twenty-six sheets of sandpaper
- Lamination paper
- Glue or glue stick
- Scissors

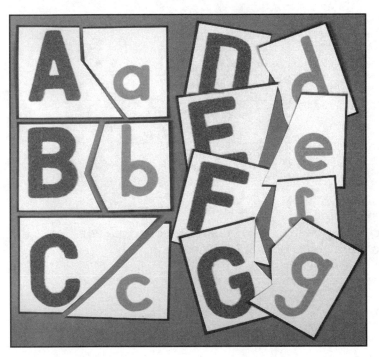

Directions

Language Arts

1. Cut 26 pieces of tagboard, 5"x 10".

2. Laminate the tagboard pieces.

3. From sandpaper or a textured fabric like corduroy, cut lower- and uppercase letters.

4. Glue an uppercase letter to the left side of the tagboard and the corresponding lowercase letter to the other side (see the accompanying photo).

5. Cut apart the pieces of tagboard using slightly different designs.

Teaching/Learning Strategies

- Place the sandpaper letters in the writing center. Encourage the children to complete the puzzles. Children can use their index fingers to trace over the letters to develop an awareness of letter formation.

Sound Drum

Developmental Goals
1. Develop auditory discrimination skills.
2. Develop a sense of rhythm.
3. Recognize patterns.

Related Curriculum Themes
Containers   Music
Instruments

Curriculum Areas
Music   Science
Language Arts

Preparation Tools and Materials
- One plastic serving tray (with deep lid)
- Jewelry beads
- Stickers
- Glue gun
- B-B pellets, paper clips, or brass fasteners
- Fun foam creatures

Language Arts

Directions
1. Place stickers, words, or pictures on the bottom of the plastic tray.
2. Place B-B pellets, jewelry beads, and fun foam creatures in the lid.
3. Attach the lid to the tray.
4. Glue around the edge of the tray and lid to seal the container.
5. Decorate the outside of the tray and lid with stickers.

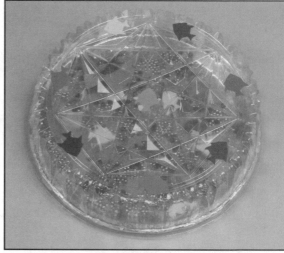

Teaching/Learning Strategies
- Introduce the sound drum during a large group activity. Encourage the children to tap a steady beat or a sound pattern. To create sound, tap the sound drum gently or tilt it back and forth.

Television Tray Chalkboard/Magnet Board

Developmental Goals

1. Enhance writing or fine motor skills.
2. Develop visual and auditory memory skills.
3. Practice retelling stories.
4. Improve small muscle coordination skills.
5. Develop eye-hand coordination skills.

Related Curriculum Themes

Symbols   Letters
Communication
Adaptable to Any Theme

Curriculum Areas

Language Arts
Music

Preparation Tools and Materials

- Metal television or serving tray
- Chalkboard spray paint
- Magnets

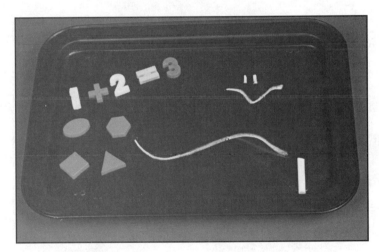

Directions

1. Spray the tray with the chalkboard paint.
2. Let the tray dry for 24 hours.
3. Decorate the border of the tray, if desired.

Teaching/Learning Strategies

- Introduce the tray to the children by demonstrating its use. Give the children chalk, chalkboard erasers, and magnetic alphabet letters to use on the tray.

Valentine Words

Developmental Goals

1. Identify Valentine's Day words.
2. Practice writing the words *heart, valentine, love, friend, card, candy, Mom,* and *Dad.*
3. Develop an awareness of the printed word.
4. Practice eye-hand coordination skills.

Related Curriculum Themes

Valentine's Day   Celebrations
Communication   Holidays
Shapes   Friendships

Curriculum Areas

Language Arts
Social Studies

Preparation Tools and Materials

- One piece of red tagboard
- Red and pink construction paper
- Manuscript or writing paper
- Markers
- Scissors (craft scissors optional)
- Glue or glue stick
- Lamination paper

Language Arts

Directions

1. Using a marker, print the title "Valentine Words" across the top of the tagboard (see the accompanying photo).

2. From construction paper, cut eight large hearts, four red and four pink. Also, cut about a dozen smaller hearts in both colors.

3. Glue the hearts to the tagboard.

4. Cut a piece of manuscript paper in heart shape to fit on each large heart, or prepare a strip by drawing two horizontal lines 1 inch apart. Measure ½ inch down from the top line and draw a row of broken lines.

5. Glue the strips of manuscript paper to the hearts.

6. On each piece of manuscript paper, print one word: *heart, Valentine, love, friend, card, candy, Mom,* and *Dad.*

7. Laminate the chart.

Teaching/Learning Strategies

- Place the chart in the writing center area. Give the children watercolor markers, pencils, crayons, and paper and encourage them to copy the chart or to write greeting cards.

- When developmentally appropriate, allow the children to prepare their own word charts. Also consider preparing word charts without words and with word cards.

Zipper Seal Bag Books

Developmental Goals

1. Develop positive self-esteem.
2. Develop small muscle skills.
3. Develop an awareness of printed words.
4. Develop expressive language skills by retelling written or drawn information.

Related Curriculum Themes

Books   My World
Art   Communication

Curriculum Areas

Language Arts
Art

Preparation Tools and Materials

- Clear zipper-seal storage bags
- Book rings
- Paper
- Markers, pencils, crayons
- Hole punch

Directions

1. Collect pages of a child or teacher made story.
2. Insert each picture or page into a zipper-seal bag.
3. Use a hole punch to create two or three holes along the top edge of the bags.
4. Bind the pages using book rings.

Teaching/Learning Strategies

- Place paper, pencils, crayons, and markers in the writing center or art area. As children make pages or pictures, create zipper-seal bag books for those who are interested. Encourage the children to read or share their books with the class or other children.

- Consider having all the children make one page to be included in a class book project.

Math

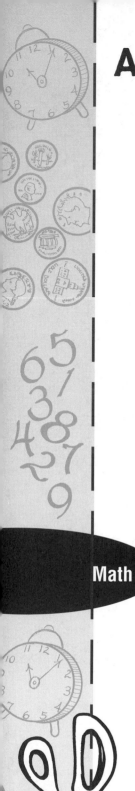

American Flag Math

Developmental Goals

1. Develop rote counting skills.
2. Identify colors.
3. Identify shapes.
4. Develop an appreciation for the American flag.
5. Develop visual discrimination skills.

Related Curriculum Themes

Fourth of July   Symbols
Flag Day   Colors
Memorial Day   Shapes
USA   Holidays
Labor Day

Curriculum Areas

Math   Social Studies
Art

Preparation Tools and Materials

- One piece of white tagboard
- Star-shaped sponge
- Red, white, and blue tempera paint
- Small paint roller

Directions

1. While discussing the American flag, begin painting a large blue square in the upper left-hand corner of the tagboard (see the accompanying photo).

2. Tell the students that there are 13 stripes on the flag (7 red and 6 white).

3. With the roller, paint 7 red stripes on the tagboard. Have the children count as you paint the stripes.

4. Next, tell the children that there are 50 stars and that each star represents a state.

5. With the star sponge and white paint, stamp 50 stars onto the blue square.

Teaching/Learning Strategies

- If desired, the children can take turns adding the stars while the group counts.
- When developmentally appropriate, allow the children to create their own flags.

Baseball and Glove Match

Developmental Goals

1. Recognize numbers.
2. Develop fine motor coordination skills.
3. Match a set of objects to a written numeral.
4. Develop eye-hand coordination skills.
5. Develop visual discrimination skills.

Related Curriculum Themes

Balls   Sports
Summer   Gloves

Curriculum Area

Math

Preparation Tools and Materials

- Brown and white tagboard
- Paper punch
- Glue or glue stick
- Black watercolor marker
- Scissors
- Lamination paper

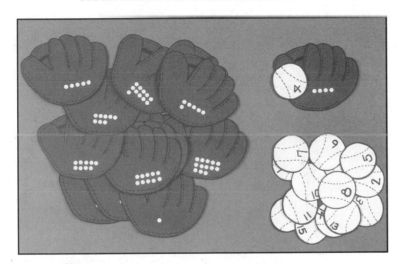

Directions

1. From the brown tagboard, trace and cut baseball-glove shapes (see the accompanying photo). Tailor the number of shapes to the developmental level of the children.

2. From the white tagboard, trace and cut the same number of baseballs.

3. On each baseball, print a different number.

4. Using a paper punch, create white dots.

5. Glue a different set of dots to each baseball glove.

6. Laminate the pieces.

Math

Teaching/Learning Strategies

- Place the gloves and balls in the math or small manipulatives area of the classroom. Encourage the children to place the ball on the glove with the corresponding number of dots.

Clock Chart

Related Curriculum Themes

Numbers   Clocks
Time

Curriculum Area

Math

Preparation Tools and Materials

- One sheet of white tagboard
- Markers
- Glue or glue stick
- Construction paper
- Numeral stencils (optional)
- Scissors
- Brass fastener
- Lamination paper

Directions

1. On the white tagboard, draw a large alarm clock shape and cut it out.

2. From the construction paper, cut 12 circles approximately 3 to 4 inches in diameter.

3. Use numeral stencils or print the numerals 1 through 12 on the circles.

4. On construction paper, draw two clock hand arrows and cut them out.

5. Laminate all pieces.

6. Use a brass fastener to attach the clock hands to the center of the clock.

Teaching/Learning Strategies

- Place the clock and number pieces in the math or small manipulatives area of the classroom. Encourage the children to put the numbers on the clock in the correct positions. Move the clock hands to match the clock in your classroom.

Math

Coin Sorting Chart

Developmental Goals

1. Practice sorting.
2. Develop visual discrimination skills.
3. Identify coins.
4. Practice counting.

Related Curriculum Themes

Money   Numbers
Shapes

Curriculum Area

Math

Preparation Tools and Materials

- One sheet of white tagboard
- Brown and gray construction paper
- Markers
- Scissors
- Glue or glue stick
- Ruler or straight edge
- Coins
- Lamination paper

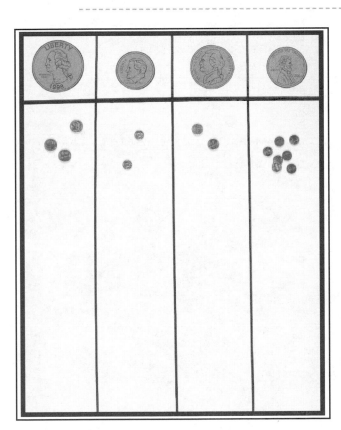

Directions

1. Use brown and gray construction paper, scissors, and markers to create quarter, dime, nickel, and penny shapes. (*Hint:* Find black-and-white masters of coin shapes. Some photocopiers accept construction paper. You can run off these coin shapes using those photocopiers.)

2. Using glue, attach the coin shapes across the top of the tagboard (see the accompanying photo).

Math

3. Using a marker and a straight edge, create a vertical column for each coin shape.

4. Laminate the chart.

Teaching/Learning Strategies

- Place the chart with a container of coins in the math or small manipulatives area of the classroom. Encourage the children to place coins in the corresponding column. The children can then count number of coins in each column. (*Note:* This activity is inappropriate for very young children because coins are a choking hazard.)

Colored Cupcakes

Developmental Goals

1. Develop visual discrimination skills.
2. Develop eye-hand coordination skills.
3. Practice using a writing tool.
4. Associate printed words with colors.

Related Curriculum Themes

Colors	Senses
Occupations	Cooking
Special Days	Writing Tools
Family	Friends
Celebrations	Breads
Food	

Curriculum Areas

Math   Social Studies

Preparation Tools and Materials

- Various colors of construction paper or tagboard
- Manuscript or writing paper
- Markers
- Scissors
- Glue or glue stick
- Lamination paper

Math

Directions

1. Cut 16 pieces of tagboard or heavy construction paper into 8" by 11" pieces, creating two sets of cards.

2. Draw a cupcake shape on each piece (see the accompanying photo).

3. For each piece of tagboard, cut a piece of manuscript writing paper. If manuscript paper is unavailable, draw lines.

4. Glue the manuscript paper to the colored sheets of paper.

5. Color each set of cupcakes a different primary or secondary color.

6. On the top manuscript line, print the name of the cupcake color.

7. On one set of cards, also print the names of the colors using dotted letters.

8. Laminate the cards.

Teaching/Learning Strategies

- Place the materials in the writing center with felt-tip markers and/or grease pencils. Encourage the children to trace the dotted letters. Once the children have done this, challenge them by providing the set without the broken lines and objects.

- Substitute other objects for the cupcakes, such as ice cream cones, cakes, shoes, balloons, jacks, balls, cards, and wagons.

Egg Count

Developmental Goals

1. Develop visual discrimination skills.
2. Develop eye-hand coordination skills.
3. Practice problem solving.
4. Associate a number of dots with a numeral.
5. Practice writing numerals.

Related Curriculum Themes

Numbers	Easter
Containers	Words
Foods	Eggs

Curriculum Areas

Social Studies   Math

Preparation Tools and Materials

- One piece of tagboard, pastel green
- Construction paper
- Manuscript paper or sentence strips
- Markers
- Paper punch
- Scissors
- Glue or glue stick
- Lamination paper

Directions

1. From different colors of construction paper, trace and cut six baskets (see the accompanying photo).
2. Glue the baskets to the tagboard.
3. Cut a strip of manuscript paper to fit on each basket or use a sentence strip.
4. On the paper or strips, glue small circles to represent the number of eggs in the basket.
5. From construction paper, cut eggs.
6. Glue a different set of eggs in each basket.
7. Laminate all pieces.
8. If desired, use a paper punch to create matching sets of small circles to glue to the manuscript paper or sentence strips.
9. Type or print the title "Egg Count" on manuscript paper or a sentence strip.
10. Using glue or a glue stick, attach the title to the tagboard sheet.
11. Laminate the chart.

Math

Teaching/Learning Strategies

- Place the egg baskets in the math or small manipulatives area of the classroom with watercolor markers or grease pencils. Encourage the children to count the eggs in each basket and to record the numbers. If necessary, demonstrate the process.

- Prepare word cards with the names of the numbers used. Depending on the developmental level of the children, increase or decrease the eggs in each basket.

Five Green Speckled Frogs Chart and Props

Developmental Goals

1. Practice counting.
2. Identify rhyming words.
3. Develop an enjoyment of music.
4. Observe printed words.

Related Curriculum Themes

Frogs	Numbers
Music	Trees
Insects	Colors

Curriculum Areas

Music	Language Arts
Math	Science

Preparation Tools and Materials

- One small piece of light blue tagboard
- Green, white, and black construction paper (or tagboard)
- Ten 1½" craft wiggle eyes
- Paper towel tube
- Brown tempera paint
- Pipe cleaners
- Markers
- Scissors (craft scissors optional)
- Glue or hot glue gun
- Tape
- Lamination paper

Math

Directions

1. On the light blue tagboard, draw a pond shape and cut it out.

2. Type or use a marker to print the following words of the song on the top portion of the pond (see the accompanying photo):

   FIVE GREEN AND SPECKLED FROGS
   Five green and speckled frogs,
   Sitting on a speckled log,
   Eating the most delicious bugs. Yum! Yum!
   One jumped into the pool,
   Where it was nice and cool,
   Now there are only four green and speckled frogs.
   (Repeat the verse, subtracting one each time.)

3. Laminate the chart.

4. Create a log prop by painting an empty paper towel tube. Decorate the log as desired.

5. To add interest, make bug shapes from construction paper.

6. Using pipe cleaners and tape or glue, attach the insect shapes to the paper towel log.

7. On green construction paper or tagboard, draw five frog shapes and cut them out.

8. Use markers to add features to the frogs.

9. Glue two craft eyes to each frog.

Five Green and Speckled Frogs

Five green and speckled frogs,
sitting on a speckled log.
Eating the most delicious bugs. Yum! Yum!
One jumped into the pool,
where it was nice and cool.
Now there are only four
green and speckled frogs.

(repeat verse subtracting one each time)

(continues)

Five Green Speckled Frogs Chart and Props

(continued)

Teaching/Learning Strategies

- Introduce the prop during a large group activity. Begin with all frog pieces on the log prop. As each verse is sung, place a frog piece on the tagboard pond. Continue singing the song until all the frogs are in the pond. After the group activity, place the props in an area for the children to use. Encourage the children to sing the song and to move the frog pieces.

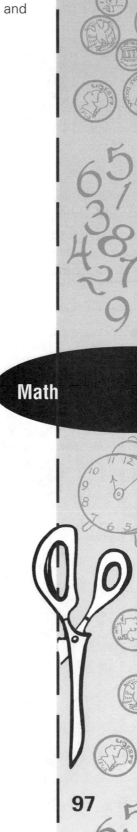

Math

Height and Weight Chart

Developmental Goals
1. Develop self-esteem.
2. Learn height and weight concepts.
3. Experience a print-rich environment.

Related Curriculum Themes
My Body   Numbers
Self-Concept

Curriculum Areas
Science   Language Arts

Preparation Tools and Materials
- One sheet of white tagboard
- Ruler
- Colored felt-tip markers
- Lamination paper

Directions

1. Across the top of the tagboard, print the title "Height and Weight Chart."

2. Using the ruler and a felt-tip marker, make three vertical columns on the chart (see the accompanying photo).

3. Label the first column "Name," the second column "Height," and the third column "Weight."

4. Using a ruler and a marker, make horizontal lines on which to record each child's name, height, and weight.

5. Laminate the chart.

Teaching/Learning Strategies

- Place a scale next to the height and weight chart. Have the children stand in front of a height chart, and record the children's names and heights on the chart. Then, weigh the children and record this data.

Math

How Many?

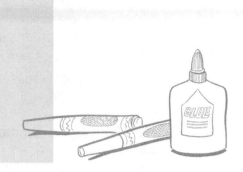

Developmental Goals

1. Recognize numbers.
2. Develop tactile discrimination.
3. Develop eye-hand coordination skills.
4. Match a set of objects to a written numeral.
5. Develop visual discrimination skills.
6. Develop problem-solving skills.
7. Develop an appreciation for printed numerals.

Related Curriculum Themes

Numbers   Communication
Sets   Senses
My World

Curriculum Areas

Math   Language Arts

Preparation Tools and Materials

- Ten tagboard cards, 4" x 6"
- Scraps of textured fabric
- Glue or hot glue gun
- Craft eyes, buttons, beans, or stickers

Directions

1. On the scraps of textured material, trace the numerals 1 through 10 and cut them out. Cut each numeral from a different textured fabric.

2. Glue the numerals to the bottom half of the tagboard cards (see the accompanying photo).

3. Glue the corresponding number of craft eyes, beans, buttons, or stickers to the top of each tagboard card.

Teaching/Learning Strategies

- Place the materials in the math or small manipulatives area of the classroom. Encourage the children to count the eyes, trace the numbers with their fingers, and identify the numbers.

- Depending on the developmental level of the children, vary the numerals to challenge the children.

Math

Ice Cream Cone Match

Developmental Goals

1. Develop visual discrimination skills.
2. Develop fine motor coordination skills.
3. Develop eye-hand coordination skills.
4. Recognize numbers.

Related Curriculum Themes

Summer Fun   Numbers
Food   Celebrations

Curriculum Areas

Math   Social Studies

Preparation Tools and Materials

- Brown, green, pink, and white tagboard
- Construction paper
- Paper punch
- Scissors
- Glue or glue stick
- Watercolor markers
- Lamination paper

Math

Directions

1. On the brown tagboard, trace ice cream cones and cut them out (see the accompanying photo).

2. On the pink, green, and white tagboard, trace ice cream scoops and cut them out.

3. Using the paper punch and construction paper, make dots.

4. Glue varying numbers of dots to the ice cream scoops.

5. On each ice cream cone, print the number that corresponds to the number of dots on the ice cream scoop.

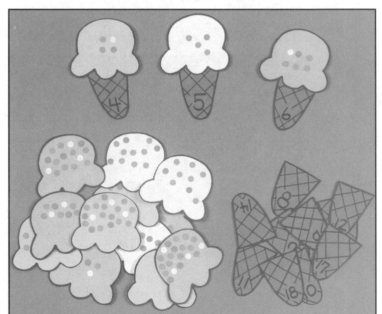

6. So that the game is self-correcting, on the back of the ice cream scoop, print the number that corresponds to the dots on the other side.

7. Laminate all pieces.

Teaching/Learning Strategies

- Place the ice cream cones in the math or small manipulatives area of the classroom. Complete a few puzzle pieces to give the children an example.

Jigsaw Puzzles

Developmental Goals

1. Develop counting skills.
2. Recognize numbers.
3. Develop one-to-one correspondence skills.
4. Develop visual discrimination skills.
5. Develop eye-hand coordination skills.
6. Develop small muscle coordination skills.
7. Develop problem-solving skills.

Related Curriculum Themes

Sizes	Numbers
Shapes	Patterns
Games	Paper
Rectangles	Colors

Curriculum Areas

Math	Language Arts

Preparation Tools and Materials

- Ten tagboard cards, 4 ½″ x 8″
- Watercolor markers
- Stickers or clip art
- Glue or glue stick
- Scissors
- Ruler
- Lamination paper

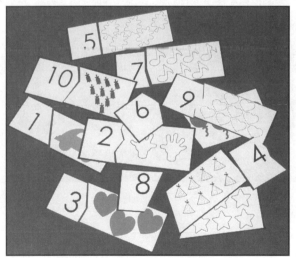

Directions

1. Divide a piece of tagboard into ten 4½″ x 9″ cards.

2. Use a watercolor marker to draw an object or place a sticker or a clip art design (see the accompanying photo). On one side of a 4½″ x 8″ card.

3. Print the number 1 on the other side of the card.

4. Continue until you have enough pieces so that the children will be challenged.

5. Laminate the cards.

6. Cut the cards apart using a different cutting pattern on each card such as zigzag, wavy, or straight edge.

Math

Teaching/Learning Strategies

- Place the materials in the math or small manipulatives area of the classroom. Encourage the children to look at the numbers, then look for the puzzle pieces with the numbers of objects. To provide the children with an example, complete a piece of the puzzle.

- Use these materials another way: Have the children sequence the number puzzles.

- When developmentally appropriate, make this activity more challenging by extending the numbers.

Make Shapes Book

Developmental Goals

1. Develop small muscle coordination skills.
2. Develop eye-hand coordination skills.
3. Develop visual discrimination skills.
4. Learn the names of basic shapes.
5. Practice making basic shapes.

Related Curriculum Theme

Shapes

Curriculum Areas

Language Arts   Math

Preparation Tools and Materials

- Construction paper or tagboard (various colors)
- Markers
- Scissors
- Lamination paper

Directions

1. Cut the construction paper or tagboard into 9" x 12" pieces.
2. On each piece, type or print a different shape name (see the accompanying photo).
3. Make the cover by printing the word "shapes" in dotted letters.
4. Decorate the cover as desired.
5. Laminate all pieces.
6. Use a book ring to store the pages together.

Teaching/Learning Strategies

- Place the materials with colored felt-tip markers in the math or small manipulatives area of the classroom. On one board, trace several shapes to show the children how the materials can be used.

Math

Mitten Number Sets

Developmental Goals

1. Develop visual discrimination skills.
2. Develop one-to-one correspondence skills.
3. Recognize numbers.
4. Develop eye-hand coordination skills.
5. Practice sequencing numbers.

Related Curriculum Themes

Counting   Numbers
Can Be Adapted to Any Theme

Curriculum Area

Math

Preparation Tools and Materials

- Pieces of tagboard, 14" x 16"
- Stickers, clip art, or magazine pictures
- Scissors
- Glue stick or hot glue gun
- Black felt-tip marker
- Lamination paper

Directions

1. From the tagboard pieces, cut a set of mitten shapes.

2. On each piece of tagboard, print a different number, repeating until enough posters have been prepared to suit the children's developmental level.

3. Glue the appropriate number of stickers or pictures to the corresponding piece of tagboard.

4. Laminate all pieces.

Math

Teaching/Learning Strategies

- Place the mittens in the math or small manipulatives area of the classroom. If needed, demonstrate how to sequence the mittens.

- Consider preparing a second set of cards to allow the children to match the numbers.

Monster Math Box

Developmental Goals

1. Develop rote counting skills.
2. Enhance number recognition.
3. Develop an understanding of number order.
4. Develop visual discrimination skills.
5. Develop eye-hand coordination skills.

Related Curriculum Themes

Halloween   Robots
Monsters   Make Believe

Curriculum Area

Math

Preparation Tools and Materials

- Shoebox
- Contact paper
- Two large wiggly eyes
- Markers
- Glue stick or glue gun
- Sharp craft knife
- Index cards
- Wiggly eye stickers

Directions

1. Cover the shoebox and lid with the contact paper.

2. With a marker, draw a large mouth on the box and cut it out.

3. Glue two large eyes to the box.

4. Add other features as desired (e.g., hair, ear, nose).

5. On index cards, print the numbers 1 through 10.

6. Place the numbers of stickers or wiggly eyes that correspond to the numbers on the cards.

Teaching/Learning Strategies

- Place the box and materials in the math or small manipulatives area of the classroom. Have a child pick an index card and look at the number of wiggly eyes and the number. Then have the child "feed the monster" the number of chips on the card.

Number Cans

Developmental Goals

1. Develop visual discrimination skills.
2. Identify written numerals.
3. Identify sets of numerals.
4. Put numbers in sequence.
5. Develop problem-solving skills.

Related Curriculum Themes

Numbers   Containers
My World

Curriculum Area

Math

Preparation Tools and Materials

- Clean, empty cans or containers with plastic lids
- Fabric or contact paper
- Stickers
- Markers
- Glue or glue stick

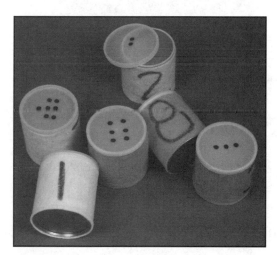

Directions

1. Cover the containers with the fabric or contact paper.
2. Using a marker, print a numeral on each can, beginning with 1.
3. Attach the lids to the cans or containers.
4. Place a set of stickers on each can or container that corresponds to the number on the container.

Teaching/Learning Strategies

- Place the number cans in the math area of the classroom. Encourage the children to identify the numbers and to put the cans in numerical order. To add interest, place in each container a corresponding set of small items, such as toy cars, jacks, or marbles, for the children to count.

Math

Number Caterpillar Puzzle

Developmental Goals

1. Identify written numerals.
2. Practice sequencing numbers.
3. Develop problem-solving skills.
4. Observe patterns.

Related Curriculum Themes

Insects   Spring
Numbers   Colors

Curriculum Areas

Math
Science

Preparation Tools and Materials

- Tagboard or
  construction paper
  (two colors)
- Marker
- Scissors
- Lamination paper

Math

Directions

1. On the tagboard or construction paper, draw a caterpillar head shape and cut it out (see the accompanying photo).

2. Using the marker, draw facial features like eyes, a nose, and a mouth on the head shape.

3. If desired, use small scraps to create antennae for the caterpillar.

4. Using scissors, cut caterpillar body segments from two colors of tagboard or construction paper.

5. On each segment, print a number with a marker, alternating colors for odd and even numbers.

6. Laminate all pieces.

Teaching/Learning Strategies

- Place the puzzle in the math or small manipulatives area of the classroom.

- If desired, vary the caterpillar puzzle. For example, make the puzzle with more or fewer body segments, depending on the level(s) of the children, or draw sets of dots on each body segment instead of numbers.

Number Line Calendar

Developmental Goals

1. Develop visual discrimination skills.
2. Recognize numbers.
3. Learn the sequence of numbers.

Related Curriculum Themes

Numbers   Symbols
Patterns   Paper

Curriculum Area

Math

Preparation Tools and Materials

- One large piece of colored tagboard
- Marker
- Scissors (craft scissors optional)
- Sentence strip, 3" x 75"
- Lamination paper

Directions

1. Cut the colored tagboard horizontally into 4" wide pieces.

2. Tape the pieces together in strips that are approximately 75" long (see the accompanying photo).

3. Using a black felt-tip marker, print the numbers 1 through 31 on the sentence strip.

4. Glue the sentence strip to the tag-board strip.

5. Laminate the combined strip.

Math

Teaching/Learning Strategies

- Attach the calendar to a wall or bulletin board at the children's eye level. Using an arrow, mark the date during group time.

- Use additional arrows or clothespins to mark holidays, birthdays, and other important dates.

Numeral Tracing Cards

Related Curriculum Themes

Writing	Sets
Letters	Numbers
Communication	Air

Curriculum Areas

Math	Language Arts

Preparation Tools and Materials

- Tagboard
- Construction paper
- Manuscript paper or sentence strips
- Watercolor markers
- Scissors
- Glue or glue stick
- Lamination paper

Directions

1. From a sheet of tagboard, cut five 9" by 12" pieces.

2. Across the top of each tagboard piece, use glue to attach a manuscript or sentence strip (see the accompanying photo).

3. Using glue, attach two sentence strips across the bottom of each tagboard piece.

4. On the manuscript line at the top of each piece of paper, print a number word, followed by its number.

5. From construction paper, cut corresponding sets of balloon shapes.

6. Glue the balloons to the tagboard pieces.

7. Using a felt-tip marker, draw strings for the balloons.

8. Using a broken line, print the number word and the number on the top manuscript line under the balloons.

9. Laminate the finished pieces.

Teaching/Learning Strategies

- Place the materials and felt-tip watercolor markers in the math or small manipulatives area of the classroom. Encourage the children to first count the balloon(s), then trace the word and corresponding numeral.

Math

Pot of Gold Count

Developmental Goals

1. Identify numbers.
2. Develop counting skills.
3. Practice following directions.
4. Match a set of objects to a written number.
5. Develop visual discrimination skills.

Related Curriculum Themes

Counting   Games
Numbers   St. Patrick's Day
Containers

Curriculum Area

Math

Preparation Tools and Materials

- Brown tagboard
- Construction paper
- Scissors
- Markers
- Glue or glue stick
- Lamination paper

Directions

1. From the tagboard, cut pot-shaped containers, creating two sets of cards (see the accompanying photo).

2. Using a marker, add details to the containers as desired.

3. On one set of the pot-shaped pieces, use a marker to print numbers on the bottoms of the pieces.

4. On the other set of pot-shaped pieces, glue corresponding sets of coin-shaped pieces to the tops of the pieces.

5. Laminate all pieces.

Math

Teaching/Learning Strategies

- Place the materials in the math or small manipulatives area of the classroom. Encourage the children to match the pot with a number with the pot with the corresponding number of coins.

- If desired, make the material self-correcting. Write the correct number on the reverse side of the pot containing the coins.

Sticker Number Cards

Developmental Goals

1. Develop visual discrimination skills.
2. Recognize numbers.
3. Practice number sequencing.
4. Practice problem solving.
5. Practice following directions.

Related Curriculum Themes

Numbers	Seasons
Words	Weather
Communication	Winter

Curriculum Areas

Math	Social Studies
Language Arts	

Preparation Tools and Materials

- Tagboard (light blue)
- Construction paper
- Snowmen figures (hand drawn, clip art, or cut from printed materials)
- Markers
- Scissors (craft scissors optional)
- Glue stick or glue gun
- Lamination paper

Math

Directions

1. From a piece of light blue tagboard, cut 5" wide horizontal strips.

2. From notepads, gift wrap, stickers, or coloring books, cut snowmen figures, or draw pictures for each strip.

3. On the first strip, paste one figure. Paste two figures on the second strip, three on the third, four on the fourth, and five on the fifth (see the accompanying photo).

4. For each strip, type or print the corresponding number and number word on construction paper and attach using glue.

5. Laminate the pieces.

Teaching/Learning Strategies

- Place the number cards in the math or writing center of the classroom. Encourage the children to count the objects on each card and to place them in numerical order.

- If appropriate, provide paper, markers, and pencils for the children to practice printing numbers and number words.

Music and Fingerplays

Apple Tree Song Chart

Developmental Goals

1. Develop an appreciation for the printed word.
2. Develop an enjoyment of music and singing.
3. Identify rhyming words.
4. Participate in a group activity.

Related Curriculum Themes

Apples   Trees
Fall   Plants
Music

Curriculum Areas

Music   Math
Language Arts

Preparation Tools and Materials

- Green tagboard
- Brown tagboard
- Construction paper or sentence strips
- Markers
- Glue or glue stick
- Scissors
- Velcro® strips or circles
- Lamination paper

Directions

1. On green tagboard, draw a large treetop shape and cut it out (see the accompanying photo).

2. On brown tagboard, draw a trunk shape and cut it out.

3. Using glue, attach the treetop to the trunk.

4. Type or use a marker to print the following title and song words on construction paper or sentence strips:

   "APPLES OFF MY TREE"
   (Sing to the tune of "Skip to My Lou")
   Pick some apples off my tree,
   Pick some apples off my tree.
   Pick some apples off my tree,
   Pick them all for you and me.

5. Using glue, attach the title and song words to the treetop shape.

6. On construction paper, draw a set of apple shapes and cut them out.

7. Laminate the tree chart and apple cutouts.

8. Using Velcro® strips or circles, attach the apple shapes to the tree.

"Apples Off My Tree"
(Sing to the tune of "Skip to My Lou")

Pick some apples off my tree,
Pick some apples off my tree,
Pick some apples off my tree,
Pick them all for you and me.

Teaching/Learning Strategies

- Use the apple tree chart as a prop when teaching the song "Apples Off My Tree." Ask a child to "pick some apples." Encourage the children to count the apples picked and the number remaining on the tree. Continue to sing the song until all children have had a turn picking apples. After group time, place the chart and apple pieces in an area of the classroom where children can use them independently.

Music and Fingerplays

Bubble Song Chart

Developmental Goals

1. Develop an appreciation for the printed word.
2. Develop an enjoyment of music and singing.
3. Identify rhyming words.
4. Associate spoken words with printed words.
5. Develop left-to-right progression skills.
6. Develop auditory and visual memory skills.
7. Develop expressive language skills.

Related Curriculum Themes

Water   Music
Bubbles

Curriculum Areas

Music
Language Arts

Preparation Tools and Materials

- One sheet of white tagboard
- Construction paper or sentence strips
- Markers
- Glue or glue stick
- Scissors (craft scissors optional)
- Lamination paper

Directions

1. Using markers, draw a turtle in a large bathtub on the white tagboard (see the accompanying photo).

2. To create interest, add bubble shapes to the drawing.

3. Type or use a marker to print the following title and song words on construction paper or sentence strips:

   "BUBBLE SONG"
   I had a little turtle,
   His name was Tiny Tim.
   I put him in the bathtub,
   To see if he could swim.
   He drank up all the water,
   He ate up all the soap.
   Now he's sick in bed,
   With a bubble in his throat.
   Bubble, bubble, bubble,
   Bubble, bubble, bubble,
   Bubble, bubble, bubble,
   Bubble, bubble, pop!

4. Using glue, attach the words to the tagboard.

5. Laminate the chart.

Teaching/Learning Strategies

- Introduce the song chart to the children during group time. Point to the words while singing the song. Encourage the children to listen for the rhyming words. Place the chart in the classroom for the children's use during choice time.

Music and Fingerplays

Cookie Jar Chart

Related Curriculum Themes

Breads   Containers
Communication   Friends

Curriculum Areas

Music   Social Studies
Language Arts

Preparation Tools and Materials

- One sheet of tagboard
- Black felt-tip marker
- Brown construction paper or tagboard
- Scissors
- Lamination paper

Directions

1. On the tagboard, draw a large cookie jar shape and cut it out (see the accompanying photo).

2. Type or use a black marker to print the following chant:

   "COOKIE JAR"
   Who took the cookies from the cookie jar?
   Who took the cookies from the cookie jar?
   Who took the cookies from the cookie jar?
   _____ took the cookies from the cookie jar.
   Who, me?
   Yes, you!
   Couldn't be!
   Then who?

3. From the brown construction paper or tagboard, cut 5" circles.

4. Print a child's name on each "cookie."

5. Laminate all pieces.

Teaching/Learning Strategies

- Using the chart, introduce the chant to the children in a small group or a large group setting. Give each child a cookie shape with the child's name printed on it. Before repeating the chant each time, ask a child to place the child's cookie on the chart. If possible, repeat the chant so that all children place their cookies on the chart.

- When appropriate, have the children print their names on their cookie shapes.

Fingerplays

Eensie Weensie Spider Chart

Developmental Goals

1. Develop an appreciation for the printed word.
2. Develop the prosocial behavior of turn taking.
3. Identify rhyming words.
4. Develop an enjoyment of music and singing.
5. Develop visual discrimination skills.
6. Associate spoken words with printed words.

Related Curriculum Themes

Spiders   Music
Summer   Water
Spring

Curriculum Areas

Music
Language Arts

Preparation Tools and Materials

- One sheet of tagboard
- Construction paper or sentence strips
- Markers
- Aluminum foil
- String
- Small spider toy
- Scissors (craft scissors optional)
- Glue or glue stick
- Ruler or straight edge
- Hole punch

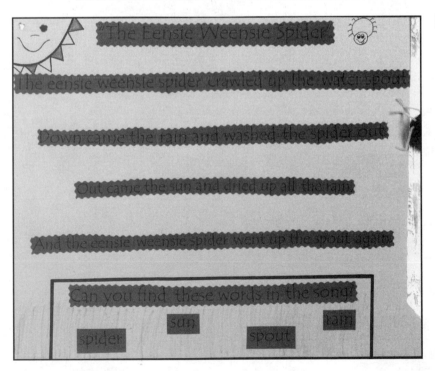

Directions

1. On the construction paper or sentence strips, type or use a marker to print the following rhyme (see the accompanying photo):

   "THE EENSIE WEENSIE SPIDER"
   The eensie weensie spider crawled up the water spout,
   Down came the rain and washed the spider out.
   Out came the sun and dried up all the rain,
   And the eensie weensie spider went up the spout again!

2. Type or use a marker to print the following questions on construction paper or sentence strips:

   Can you find these words in the song?
   Spider? Sun? Spout? Rain?

3. Using glue, attach the song words to the tagboard.

4. Using glue, attach the questions to the bottom of the tagboard.

5. Using a marker and ruler, create a box around the question and words.

6. Using markers, draw a picture of a sun in the upper left corner of the tagboard.

Music and Fingerplays

(continues)

Eensie Weensie Spider Chart

(continued)

7. Cut a 2½" long piece of aluminum foil and glue it to the right edge of the tagboard.

8. Laminate the chart.

9. Using a hole punch, create a small hole at the top of the piece of aluminum foil.10. Cut and tie a piece of string around the toy spider.

11. Insert the string through the hole.

Teaching/Learning Strategies

• Introduce the song chart to the children in a large group setting. Pull on the string to make the spider "go up the water spout." Release the string to "wash the spider out." Place the song chart in the classroom so that the children can use the chart during self-selection time.

Music and Fingerplays

116

Finding Colors Song Chart

Developmental Goals

1. Develop an appreciation for the printed word.
2. Identify colors.
3. Develop visual discrimination skills.
4. Develop an enjoyment of music and singing.
5. Associate spoken words with printed words.

Related Curriculum Themes

Colors   School
Music

Curriculum Areas

Music   Science
Language Arts

Preparation Tools and Materials

- One sheet of tagboard
- Construction paper or sentence strips
- Markers
- Glue or glue stick
- Scissors (craft scissors optional)
- Tape
- Lamination paper

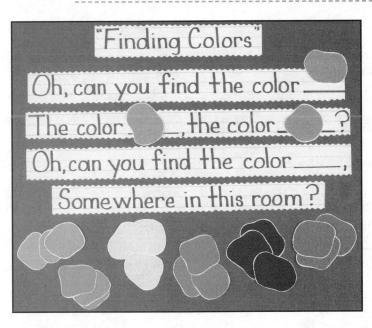

Directions

1. On the construction paper or sentence strips, type or use a marker to print the following title, supply list, and directions (see the accompanying photo):

   "FINDING COLORS"
   Oh, can you find the color _____?
   The color _____, the color _____?
   Oh, can you find the color _____?
   Somewhere in this room?

2. Using glue, attach the word to the tagboard.

3. From each color of construction paper, cut four irregularly rounded shapes.

4. Laminate the chart and color shapes.

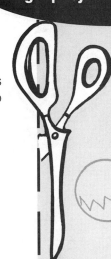

Music and Fingerplays

Teaching/Learning Strategies

- Use the chart and pieces during group time. Tape identically colored pieces to the blank areas of the chart. Sing the "Finding Colors" song to the tune of "Muffin Man." Ask the children to find objects in the room that are the same color mentioned in the song. To continue, remove the colored pieces and tape another set of colored pieces on the chart.

Little Petals Song Chart

Developmental Goals

1. Develop an appreciation for the printed word.
2. Practice counting.
3. Develop an enjoyment of music and singing.
4. Associate spoken words with printed words.
5. Develop visual discrimination skills.

Related Curriculum Themes

Flowers   Gardens
Plants   Numbers

Curriculum Areas

Music   Language Arts
Math

Preparation Tools and Materials

- One sheet of light blue tagboard
- Construction paper or sentence strips
- Markers
- Glue or glue stick
- Scissors
- Lamination paper

Directions

1. Using the construction paper and scissors, create flower parts (see the accompanying photo). Include a stem, leaf, and 10 petals.

2. Using glue, attach the stem, leaf, and flower center to the light blue tagboard. Do not glue the petals to the tagboard.

3. On construction paper or sentence strips, type or use a marker to print the following words of the "Little Petals" song:

   LITTLE PETALS
   One little, two little, three little petals,
   Four little, five little, six little petals.
   Seven little, eight little, nine little
    petals,
   Ten petals growing on a stem!

4. Using glue, attach the song words to the center of the flower.

5. If desired, add facial features to the flower and grass along the lower edge of the tagboard.

6. Laminate the chart.

Teaching/Learning Strategies

- Place the song chart and flower petals on a table or the floor. Sing the song to the tune of "Ten Little Indians." Encourage the children to place the petals on the flower as they are counted in the song. Allow the children to use the song chart during self-selection time.

Penguin Song Chart

Developmental Goals

1. Develop visual discrimination skills.
2. Identify rhyming words.
3. Associate spoken words with printed words.
4. Develop an enjoyment of music and singing.
5. Develop left-to-right progression skills.
6. Develop auditory and visual memory skills.

Related Curriculum Themes

Birds   Winter
Music   Colors

Curriculum Areas

Music   Language Arts
Science

Preparation Tools and Materials

- One sheet of black tagboard
- White and orange construction paper
- Markers
- Scissors
- Glue or glue stick
- Lamination paper

Romp and Play
Sung to "Twinkle, Twinkle, Little Star"
Watch the penguins romp and play,
Sliding on the ice all day.
Dressed in coats of black and white,
They are such a funny sight.
Watch the penguins as they play.
On a cold, cold winter day.

Directions

1. On the black tagboard, draw a large penguin shape and cut it out (see the accompanying photo).

2. Using orange construction paper, create a beak and feet.

3. Using glue, attach the beak and feet to the penguin shape.

4. Using white construction paper, create eyes, a tie, and a stomach.

5. Using glue, attach the eyes, tie, and stomach to the penguin shape.

6. Type or use a marker to print the following song words on the penguin shape:

    ROMP AND PLAY
    (SUNG TO "TWINKLE, TWINKLE, LITTLE STAR")
    Watch the penguins romp and play,
    Sliding on the ice all day.
    Dressed in coats of black and white,
    They are such a funny sight.
    Watch the penguins as they play.
    On a cold, cold winter day.

7. Laminate the chart.

Teaching/Learning Strategies

- Use the "Romp and Play" chart as a prop for teaching the song. Point to the words as they are sung. Place the chart in the classroom for the children's use during free choice time.

Music and Fingerplays

Popcorn Song Chart

Developmental Goals

1. Develop an enjoyment of music and singing.
2. Develop an appreciation for the printed word.
3. Associate spoken words with printed words.
4. Identify rhyming words.
5. Develop left-to-right progression skills.

Related Curriculum Themes

Food   Senses
Friends   Cooking

Curriculum Areas

Music   Science
Language Arts

Preparation Tools and Materials

- One sheet of white tagboard
- Markers
- Scissors
- Lamination paper

Directions

1. On the tagboard, draw a large popcorn kernel shape and cut it out (see the accompanying photo).

2. Type or use a marker to print the following title and song words on the tagboard:

   "POPCORN SONG"
   (SUNG TO THE TUNE OF "I'M A LITTLE TEAPOT")
   I'm a little popcorn in a pot.
   Heat me up and watch me pop.
   When I get all fat and white,
   Then I'm done.
   Popping corn is lots of fun.

3. Laminate the chart.

> **"Popcorn Song"**
> (Sung to the tune of "I'm a Little Teapot")
>
> I'm a little popcorn in a pot.
> Heat me up and watch me pop.
> When I get all fat and white,
> then I'm done.
> Popping corn is lots of fun.

Teaching/Learning Strategies

- Use the chart to help teach the "Popcorn Song" to the children. Point to each word as it is sung. Encourage children to do actions and movements to the song. Afterward, make popcorn.

Music and Fingerplays

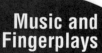

Pumpkin Poem Chart

Developmental Goals

1. Develop an appreciation for the printed word.
2. Identify rhyming words.
3. Develop visual and auditory memory skills.
4. Associate spoken words with printed words.
5. Develop left-to-right progression skills.

Related Curriculum Themes

Pumpkins	Gardens
Halloween	Plants
Colors	Feelings

Curriculum Areas

Language Arts   Music

Preparation Tools and Materials

- One sheet of orange tagboard
- Brown and green construction paper
- Markers
- Scissors (craft scissors optional)
- Glue or glue stick
- Lamination paper

Directions

1. On the orange tagboard, draw a large pumpkin shape and cut it out (see the accompanying photo).

2. Using the brown construction paper, make a stem shape.

3. Using glue, attach the stem to the pumpkin shape.

4. Using the green construction paper, make a vine leaf shape.

5. Using glue, attach the vine leaf to the pumpkin shape.

6. On the construction paper or sentence strips, type or use a marker to print the following title and poem:

"I'm a Little Pumpkin"
I'm a little pumpkin, orange and round.
When I'm sad, my face wears a frown.
But when I'm happy and all a glow,
Watch my smile just grow and grow!

7. Use glue to attach the poem strips to the tagboard pumpkin.

8. Laminate the chart.

Teaching/Learning Strategies

- Introduce the poem chart to the children during group time. As the poem is recited, point to the words. This poem can also be sung to the tune of "I'm a Little Teapot." After group time, place the chart in the classroom for the children's use during choice time.

Music and Fingerplays

Three Brown Mice Flannel Board Song

Developmental Goals
1. Develop an enjoyment of music and songs.
2. Practice counting.
3. Identify rhyming words.
4. Develop auditory memory skills.

Related Curriculum Themes
Mice   Animals
Colors   Music
Cats

Curriculum Areas
Music   Language Arts
Math

Preparation Tools and Materials
- Felt pieces—black, dark brown, brown, tan, white, and pink
- Scissors
- Glue or hot glue gun
- Pipe cleaners
- Small wiggle eyes
- Yarn

Directions
1. From a piece of black felt, cut a cat's head (see the accompanying photo).
2. From pink felt, cut pink triangles to represent the cat's ears and nose.
3. Using glue or the hot glue gun, attach the pieces to the black cat's head.
4. Using white and black felt, make the cat's eyes.
5. Attach the pieces to the cat's face.
6. Using pieces of yarn, create a mouth shape.
7. Attach the yarn to the cat's face.
8. Cut pipe cleaners to represent the cat's whiskers.
9. Attach the whiskers to the cat's face.
10. From the brown pieces of felt, cut three mice shapes.
11. From pink felt, cut half circles to represent the mouse ears.
12. From pink felt, also cut small triangles for the mouse noses.
13. Attach the mouse pieces with glue.
14. Using pipe cleaners, make mouse legs and tails.
15. Attach the pipe cleaners with glue.
16. Using pieces of yarn, create mouse mouths.
17. Attach the mouse mouths with glue.
18. Glue small wiggle eyes to each mouse's head.

Music and Fingerplays

"Three Brown Mice"
(Sung to the tune of "Three Blind Mice")
Three brown mice, three brown mice.
See how they run. See how they run.
They were chased through the house by the big black cat.
Lucky for them, she was lazy and fat.
Did you ever see such a sight as that?
Three brown mice, three brown mice.

(continues)

Three Brown Mice Flannel Board Song

(contined)

Teaching/Learning Strategies

- Use the cat and mouse pieces on a flannel board to help teach the following song, "Three Brown Mice," which is sung to the tune of "Three Blind Mice":

  Three brown mice, three brown mice,
  See how they run. See how they run.
  They were chased through the house by the big black cat.
  Lucky for them, she was lazy and fat.
  Did you ever see such a sight as that?
  Three brown mice, three brown mice.

- Leave the pieces out for the children to use and practice the song.

- Make sets of differently colored mice to change the words of the song and highlight other colors.

Two Little Apples Chart

Developmental Goals

1. Develop an appreciation for the printed word.
2. Identify rhyming words.
3. Develop visual and auditory memory skills.
4. Develop expressive language skills.
5. Associate spoken words with written words.

Related Curriculum Themes

Apples   Fall
Fruit   Numbers
Trees

Curriculum Areas

Language Arts   Math
Science

Preparation Tools and Materials

- One sheet of white tagboard
- One sheet of green tagboard
- One sheet of brown tagboard
- Construction paper or sentence strips
- Markers
- Scissors (craft scissors optional)
- Glue or glue stick
- Tape
- Lamination paper

Directions

1. On the green tagboard, draw a large treetop shape and cut it out (see the accompanying photo).

2. On the brown tagboard, draw a large tree trunk shape and cut it out.

3. Using glue or tape, attach the trunk to the treetop shape.

4. Using red construction paper, create two apple shapes.

5. Decorate the apples as desired, and tape or glue them to the upper area of the treetop.

6. Type or use a marker to print the following title and words of the apple poem on construction paper or sentence strips:

   TWO LITTLE APPLES
   Two little apples hanging high in a tree.
   Two little apples smiling at me.
   I shook that tree as hard as I could.
   Down came the apples.
   Mmmmmm, so good.

7. Using glue, attach the words to the white tagboard.

8. Laminate the chart.

Two Little Apples

Two little apples hanging high in a tree.
Two little apples smiling at me.
I shook that tree as hard as I could.
Down came the apples.
Mmmmmmm, so good.

Teaching/Learning Strategies

- Introduce the apples fingerplay to the children during group time. As the fingerplay is recited, point to the words on the chart. After group time, place the chart in the classroom for the children's use during choice time.

Music and Fingerplays

Science

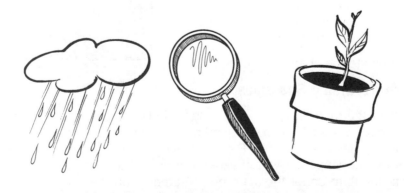

Absorption Chart

Developmental Goals

1. Learn the new vocabulary word *absorption*.
2. Practice predicting.
3. Learn science concepts.
4. Associate objects with printed words.
5. Develop an appreciation for the printed word.
6. Develop left-to-right progression skills.

Related Curriculum Themes
Water
Science

Curriculum Areas
Science
Language Arts

Preparation Tools and Materials
- One sheet of white tagboard
- Tagboard or construction paper pieces, 10" x 2½"
- Markers
- Ruler
- Lamination paper

Directions

1. Print the words "Absorption Chart" across the top of the tagboard (see the accompanying photo).

2. Under the title, print the following: "Place drops of water on the items. What happens?"

3. Using a ruler and marker, divide the remaining sheet of tagboard in half.

4. On the left side, print the words "These items absorb water."

5. On the right side, print the words "These items do not absorb water."

6. On 10" x 2½" pieces of tagboard, draw symbols and print their names. Include symbols for paper towel, sponge, wax paper, aluminum foil, yarn, cotton ball, cork, towel, bottle cap, paper, tissue, wood chip, and a penny.

7. Laminate the chart and pieces.

Absorption Chart

Place drops of water on the items. What happens?

☺These items absorb water.

☹These items do not absorb water.

paper towel
sponge

wax paper
aluminum foil

yarn
cotton ball
cork   towel
bottle cap
paper   tissue
woodchip
penny

Teaching/Learning Strategies

- Collect the materials for the activity, including paper towels, sponge, yarn, a cotton ball, cork, a kitchen towel, waxed paper, aluminum foil, a bottle cap, a paper, tissue, a penny, and a wood chip. Place drops of water on each item. Observe. Ask the children what happens. As you experiment with each item, have a child place the card with the item under the appropriate category on the chart.

Circle Glider Chart

Developmental Goals

1. Develop an appreciation for the printed word.
2. Practice following directions.
3. Practice predicting.
4. Associate spoken words with printed words.
5. Observe the movement of an object through air.
6. Develop left-to-right progression skills.
7. Develop problem-solving skills.

Related Curriculum Themes

Shapes   Air
Movement   Science

Curriculum Areas

Science
Language Arts

Preparation Tools and Materials

- One sheet of white tagboard
- One strip of construction paper, 9" x 1"
- One strip of construction paper, 6" x 1"
- Construction paper or sentence strips
- Plastic drinking straw
- Two paper clips
- Glue or glue stick
- Black felt-tip marker

Make a circle glider.

You will need:

9" x 1" strip
6" x 1" strip
straw
2 paper clips

Make a loop with each strip.

Attach the loops to the straw using the paper clips.

Sail the glider through the air with the small loop in front.

Directions

1. On the construction paper or sentence strips, type or use a marker to print the following directions for making a circle glider (see the accompanying photo):

   ### MAKE A CIRCLE GLIDER

   a. You will need:
      - 9" x 1" strip
      - 6" x 1" strip
      - Straw
      - Two paper clips

   b. Make a loop with each strip.
   c. Attach the loops to the straw using the paper clips.
   d. Sail the glider through the air with the small loop in front.

2. Using glue, attach the directions to the tagboard.

3. Glue the paper strips, straw, and paper clips to the chart using the accompanying photo as a guide.

Teaching/Learning Strategies

- Display the chart above a table with the necessary materials. After the children make the circle gliders, they can use the gliders outdoors or in a large indoor area.

Science

127

Fruit Drink Taste Test Chart

Developmental Goals

1. Develop an appreciation for the printed word.
2. Practice collecting and recording data.
3. Develop beginning graphing skills.
4. Recognize the concepts of more or fewer.
5. Practice discriminating between and among different flavors.

Related Curriculum Themes

Senses or Sense of Taste
Fruits   Colors
Summer

Curriculum Areas

Science   Language Arts
Math

Preparation Tools and Materials

- One sheet of tagboard (dark blue)
- Construction paper or sentence strips
- Packages of fruit drink mixes
- Scissors (craft scissors optional)
- Glue or glue stick
- Markers
- Ruler or straight edge
- Lamination paper

Directions

1. On the construction paper or sentence strips, type or use a marker to print the title "Fruit Drink Taste Test" and the question "What's Your Favorite Flavor?"

2. Using glue, attach the strips horizontally across the top of the tagboard (see the accompanying photo).

3. Using a ruler or straight edge and a marker, draw a horizontal line under the chart captions.

4. Cut pictures from the front sides of fruit drink mix packages.

5. Using glue, attach the package pictures horizontally below the chart captions on the tagboard.

6. Below each picture, print the name of the fruit mix flavor.

7. Using a marker and ruler, vertically divide the chart into columns.

8. Laminate the chart.

Teaching/Learning Strategies

- Prepare various flavors of fruit drinks for the children to sample. Encourage the children to choose a favorite flavor. The children can then use watercolor markers to print their names on the chart in the columns for their favorite flavors. After all the children have participated, the class can determine how many people liked each flavor. Use such math vocabulary words as *more, less, most, fewer,* and *same* to help the children explain the data they have gathered.

Favorite Vegetable Chart

Developmental Goals

1. Practice sorting.
2. Develop an appreciation for the printed word.
3. Develop matching skills.
4. Identify one's name in print.

Related Curriculum Themes

Vegetables	Plants
Summer	Seeds
Gardens	Colors

Curriculum Areas

Science	Language Arts
Math	

Preparation Tools and Materials

- One sheet of tagboard (green)
- Construction paper
- Six packages of vegetable seeds
- Markers
- Scissors
- Glue or glue stick
- Ruler or straight edge
- Tape
- Lamination paper

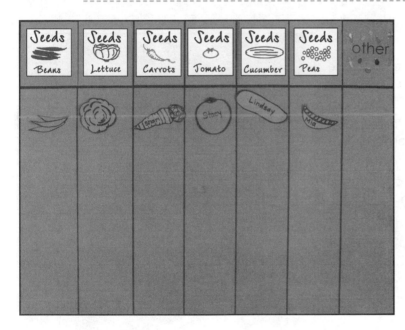

Directions

1. Cut the front labels off the vegetable seed packets.

2. Using glue or a glue stick, attach the labels along the top of the tagboard, leaving a 3-inch space at the end (see the accompanying photo).

3. In the space remaining on the chart, type or use a marker to print the word "other."

4. Using a marker and straight edge, create a vertical column for each label.

5. Laminate the chart.

6. If desired, draw and cut sets of matching vegetable shapes for the children's names.

Science

Teaching/Learning Strategies

- Introduce the chart to the children in a large group setting. The children can choose vegetable shapes that match their favorite vegetables. If necessary, help the children print their names on the vegetable shapes. Use tape to attach vegetables with names to the corresponding columns. After the chart is complete, have the children help count the children who like beans, carrots, tomatoes, and so on.

Fruits and Vegetables Sorting Chart

Developmental Goals

1. Identify fruits and vegetables.
2. Develop visual discrimination skills.
3. Develop problem-solving skills.
4. Develop eye-hand coordination skills.
5. Develop fine motor coordination skills.

Related Curriculum Themes

Foods   Garden
Fruits   Plants
Vegetables

Curriculum Areas

Science   Math

Preparation Tools and Materials

- One sheet of tagboard (yellow)
- Markers
- Glue or glue stick
- Construction paper or sentence strips
- Ruler or straight edge
- Small plastic fruits and vegetables
- Lamination paper

Directions

1. On the construction paper or sentence strips, type or use a marker to print the words "Fruits" and "Vegetables."

2. Using a ruler and a marker, divide the sheet of tagboard in half vertically (see the accompanying photo).

3. Using glue, attach the word "Fruits" to the top left of the tagboard.

4. Using glue, attach the word "Vegetables" to the top right of the tagboard.

5. Using a ruler and a marker, draw a horizontal line below the words.

6. Laminate the chart.

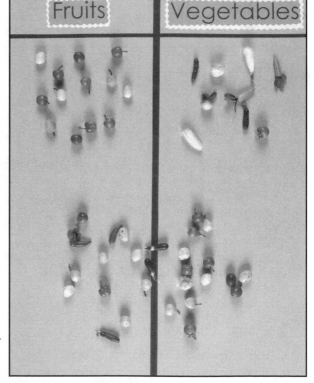

Teaching/Learning Strategies

- Place the chart and plastic fruit and vegetable pieces on the floor or on a table in the small manipulatives area of the classroom. Encourage the children to place the fruits on the left side of the chart and the vegetables on the right side of the chart. Also consider using pictures of fruits and vegetables for sorting.

Science

Handwashing Chart

Developmental Goals

1. Practice good hygiene by following correct hand-washing procedures.
2. Develop an appreciation for the printed word.
3. Practice following directions.
4. Develop self-help skills.

Related Curriculum Themes

My Body   Bubbles
Water

Curriculum Areas

Science   Language Arts
Health

Preparation Tools and Materials

- One sheet of white tagboard
- Construction paper or sentence strips
- Felt
- Markers
- Glue or glue stick
- Scissors

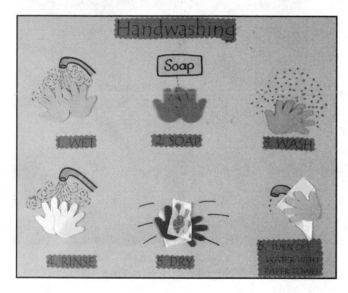

Directions

1. On the construction paper or sentence strips, type or use a marker to print the following chart caption and procedures (see the accompanying photo):

   HANDWASHING
   1. Wet
   2. Soap
   3. Wash
   4. Rinse
   5. Dry
   6. Turn off water with paper towel

2. Using glue, attach the caption to the top of the tagboard.

3. Using glue, attach the procedure words to the tagboard sequentially.

4. Cut hand shapes from felt.

5. Using markers and the hand shapes on the tagboard, illustrate the procedures.

Teaching/Learning Strategies

- Introduce the handwashing chart to the children during group time. Explain all steps, and allow the children to practice the steps. Display the sign by the sink in your classroom. Refer to the chart as needed.

Science

Listening Cards

Developmental Goals

1. Develop listening skills.
2. Distinguish sound differences (loud or soft).
3. Develop visual and auditory memory.
4. Develop visual discrimination skills.
5. Identify and match sounds with pictures.
6. Practice problem solving.

Related Curriculum Themes

Five Senses   Music

Curriculum Areas

Science   Language Arts

Preparation Tools and Materials

- Magazines
- Scissors
- Glue or glue stick
- Card stock, 4" x 6"
- Tape recorder
- Blank cassette tape
- Lamination paper

Directions

1. Obtain pictures for the listening cards that can be easily identified with a sound (e.g., water running, a dog barking, a baby crying, a doorbell ringing, a car horn beeping) in one of three ways: (1) print computer clip art, (2) use magazine pictures, or (3) use a digital camera.

2. Glue the pictures to 4" x 6" card stock.

3. Laminate the cards.

4. Record a sound for each picture.

Teaching/Learning Strategies

- During large group time, introduce sounds and have the children find the associated pictures. After group time, place the materials in a classroom area for the children's independent use. To help the children turn the tape recorder on and off, cut green and red circles from construction paper. Tape the green circle on the play button and the red circle on the stop button.

Science

Magic Mirror Pictures

Developmental Goals

1. Develop visual discrimination skills.
2. Learn that a mirror creates a reflection.
3. Practice predicting.

Related Curriculum Themes

I'm Special   Sense of Sight
Pictures

Curriculum Area

Science

Preparation Tools and Materials

- Colored tagboard squares, 6" x 6"
- White construction paper squares, 5" x 5"
- Colored felt-tip markers
- Scissors
- Glue or glue stick
- Lamination paper

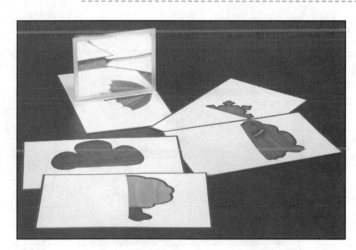

Directions

1. On a 5" x 5" piece of white construction paper, draw half an object (e.g., a face, a star, a fish, a rainbow, a dress, a butterfly, an ice cream cone, or a heart) (see the accompanying photo).

2. Using glue, mount the 5" x 5" square on a 6" x 6" piece of colored tagboard.

3. Laminate the cards.

Teaching/Learning Strategies

- Make discovery or science activities available daily for children's use during self-directed periods. Place the magic mirror pictures on a table, and give the children a mirror. Demonstrate how to place the mirror on the edge of the pictures. The picture will reflect in the mirror and look whole.

- Consider varying the sizes of the pictures.

- When developmentally appropriate, have the children prepare their own magic mirror pictures as an activity.

Science

Match the Blocks Chart

Developmental Goals

1. Develop visual discrimination skills.
2. Practice matching.
3. Develop eye-hand coordination skills.
4. Develop problem-solving skills.

Related Curriculum Themes

Blocks   School
Shapes   Construction

Curriculum Areas

Science
Math

Preparation Tools and Materials

- One sheet of dark tagboard (red, blue, or green)
- White construction paper
- Markers
- Scissors
- Glue or glue stick
- Unit blocks
- Lamination paper

Directions

1. On the construction paper or a sentence strip, type or use a marker to print the caption "Match the Blocks."

2. Using glue, attach the caption to the top of the tagboard (see the accompanying photo).

3. On the white construction paper, trace shapes of unit blocks and cut them out.

4. Using glue, attach the block shapes to the tagboard.

5. Laminate the chart.

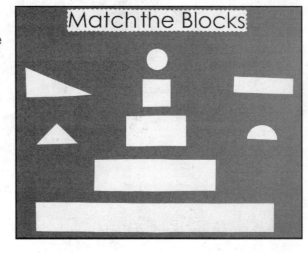

Teaching/Learning Strategies

- Place the chart on the floor near the unit blocks. Encourage the children to find blocks to match the paper shapes and to place the blocks on the chart.

Science

Movement Jars

Developmental Goals
1. Develop observation skills.
2. Develop prediction skills.
3. Develop visual discrimination skills.
4. Note differences and likenesses.

Related Curriculum Themes
Movement
Water

Curriculum Areas
Science
Language Arts

Preparation Tools and Materials
- Five jars with lids, 6 or 8 ounce
- Six marbles
- Clear liquids (water, vegetable oil, corn syrup, saltwater, glycerin, and baby oil)
- Construction paper or tagboard
- Rubber cement or hot glue gun
- Watercolor marker
- Lamination paper

Directions
1. Fill each jar with a different type of clear liquid.
2. Add a marble to each jar.
3. Using rubber cement or a hot glue gun, glue the lids securely on the jars.
4. On the construction paper or tagboard, type or use a marker to print the question, "Which moves the fastest? Slowest?"
5. Laminate the chart.

Teaching/Learning Strategies
- During group time, introduce the five movement jars. Encourage the children to take turns exploring and turning each jar. The children can observe the movement of the object as they turn each jar. Ask the children to describe their observations. Then, have the children order the jars from fastest to slowest.

- Repeat the activity using only one medium but other objects, such as a stone, paper clips, beads, sequins, or pennies.

- *Note:* Take care when using glass jars.

Science

Ocean Creatures Lacing Cards

Developmental Goals

1. Develop small muscle coordination.
2. Practice eye-hand coordination.
3. Develop visual discrimination skills.
4. Identify sea animals.

Related Curriculum Themes

Ocean   Beach
Water   Summer
Creatures of the Sea

Curriculum Areas

Science
Language Arts

Preparation Tools and Materials

- Tagboard (various colors)
- Yarn, string, or shoelaces
- Markers
- Hole punch
- Lamination paper

Directions

1. On the colored tagboard, draw a turtle, a starfish, a lobster, a dolphin, and a seahorse and cut them out (see the accompanying photo).

2. Using a marker, add such details as eyes, noses, and mouths to the creatures, and print the creatures' names.

3. Laminate all pieces.

4. Using a hole punch, create a series of holes around the edges of all pieces.

Teaching/Learning Strategies

- Place the lacing cards in the small manipulatives area of the classroom. To prevent loss, tie one end of a lace to each card. Encourage the children to lace around the cards.

Recipe Chart: Banana Bobs

Developmental Goals

1. Develop an appreciation for the printed word.
2. Associate spoken words with written words.
3. Practice following directions.
4. Develop eye-hand coordination skills.

Related Curriculum Themes

Foods   Cooking
Fruits   Friends

Curriculum Areas

Science
Language Arts

Preparation Tools and Materials

- One sheet of tagboard (yellow)
- Construction paper or sentence strips
- Scissors (craft scissors optional)
- Glue or glue stick
- Markers
- Stickers or clip art
- Lamination paper

Banana Bobs

Cut bananas into chunks.

Dip into honey.

Roll in wheat germ.

Use large toothpicks for serving.

Directions

1. On the construction paper or sentence strips, type or use a marker to print the following title and recipe directions (see the accompanying photo):

   BANANA BOBS
   Cut bananas into chunks.
   Dip into honey.
   Roll in wheat germ.
   Use large toothpicks for serving.

2. Using glue, attach the title and directions to the tagboard, leaving a few inches between steps.

3. Using construction paper and markers, illustrate each step of the recipe.

4. Decorate the chart with stickers or clip art as desired.

5. Laminate the chart.

Teaching/Learning Strategies

- Collect the ingredients and supplies for making Banana Bobs. Hang the recipe chart near the preparation area. Refer to the chart for step-by-step directions. Have the children make Banana Bobs for a snack.

Science

Recipe Chart: Dog Biscuits

Developmental Goals

1. Develop an appreciation for the printed word.
2. Practice following directions.
3. Observe changes in substances.
4. Associate spoken words with written words.
5. Develop left-to-right progression skills.
6. Develop eye-hand coordination skills.

Related Curriculum Themes

Dogs   Family
Pets   Friends
Cooking

Curriculum Areas

Science   Language Arts
Math

Preparation Tools and Materials

- Two sheets of tagboard
- Construction paper or sentence strips
- Scissors
- Glue or glue stick
- Markers
- Lamination paper

Directions

1. On one of the tagboard sheets using markers and scissors, draw a large dog shape and cut it out (see the accompanying photo). Include such details as eyes, a nose, a mouth, and a collar.

2. On construction paper, type or use a marker to print the following ingredients for making dog biscuits.

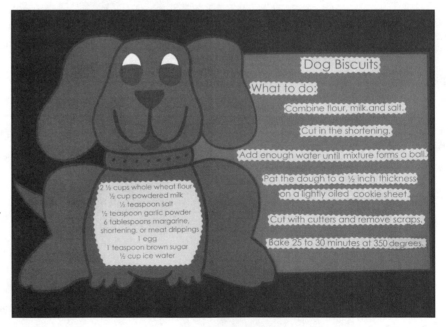

   2½ cups whole wheat flour
   ½ cup powdered milk
   ½ teaspoon salt
   ½ teaspoon garlic powder
   6 tablespoons margarine, shortening, or meat drippings
   1 egg
   1 teaspoon brown sugar
   ½ cup ice water

3. Using glue, attach the ingredient list to the dog shape.

4. Type or use a marker to print the following title and procedures on construction paper or sentence strips:

(continues)

Science

Recipe Chart: Dog Biscuits

(continued)

DOG BISCUITS
WHAT TO DO:
Combine flour, milk, and salt.
Cut in the shortening.
Add enough water until mixture forms a ball.
Pat the dough to a ½-inch thickness on a lightly oiled cookie sheet.
Cut with cutters and remove scraps.
Bake 25 to 30 minutes at 350 degrees.

5. Using glue, attach the title and directions to the second sheet of tagboard.
6. Using glue, attach the dog shape to the outer edge of the second sheet of tagboard.
7. Laminate the chart.

Teaching/Learning Strategies

- Gather the ingredients and tools for making dog biscuits. Place the dog biscuit chart near where you will be working. Refer to the chart for step-by-step procedures. Encourage the children to help make dog biscuits, and donate the biscuits to an animal shelter.

Science

Recipe Chart: Gingerbread Boy

Developmental Goals

1. Develop an appreciation for the printed word.
2. Practice beginning measuring skills.
3. Develop prediction skills.
4. Observe changes in substances.
5. Associate spoken words with written words.
6. Develop left-to-right progression skills.
7. Develop eye-hand coordination skills.

Related Curriculum Themes

Breads   Shapes
Cooking   Friends
Families

Curriculum Areas

Science   Language Arts
Math

Preparation Tools and Materials

- One sheet of brown tagboard
- Construction paper
- Markers
- Scissors (craft scissors optional)
- Glue or glue stick
- Lamination paper

Directions

1. On the brown tagboard, draw a large gingerbread person and cut it out (see the accompanying photo).

2. Using construction paper and scissors, create eyes, nose, mouth, and button shapes.

3. Glue the shapes to the gingerbread person shape.

4. Type or use a marker to print the following recipe for gingerbread shapes:

   1½ cups whole wheat flour
   1 teaspoon baking soda
   ½ teaspoon salt
   ½ teaspoon ginger
   1 teaspoon cinnamon
   ¼ cup oil
   ¼ cup maple syrup
   ¼ cup honey
   1 large egg

1 ½ cups whole-wheat flour
1 teaspoon baking soda
½ teaspoon salt
½ teaspoon ginger
1 teaspoon cinnamon
¼ cup oil
¼ cup maple syrup
¼ cup honey
1 large egg

Make a Gingerbread Boy

Preheat oven to 350 degrees.
Measure all of the dry ingredients into a bowl and mix well.
Measure all wet ingredients into a second bowl and mix well.
Add the two mixtures together.
Pour the combined mixture into an 8-inch square pan
and bake for 30 to 35 minutes.
When cool, roll the gingerbread dough into thin slices.
Cut out gingerbread people.
Decorate and ENJOY!

Science

140   *(continues)*

Recipe Chart: Gingerbread Boy

(continued)

MAKE A GINGERBREAD BOY

Preheat the oven to 350 degrees. Measure all the dry ingredients into a bowl and mix well. Measure all wet ingredients into a second bowl and mix well. Add the two mixtures. Pour the combined mixture into an 8-inch square pan and bake 30 to 35 minutes. When cool, roll the gingerbread dough into thin slices. Cut out gingerbread people. Decorate and enjoy!

5. Laminate the chart.

Teaching/Learning Strategies

- Collect the ingredients for gingerbread boys. Hang the chart near the preparation area. Refer to the chart for step-by-step directions. Serve the cookies for snack or dessert.

Science

Recipe Chart: Macaroni and Cheese

Developmental Goals

1. Develop an appreciation for the printed word.
2. Practice following directions.
3. Associate spoken words with written words.
4. Observe changes in substances.
5. Develop left-to-right progression skills.

Related Curriculum Themes

Foods   Noodles/Pasta
Cooking   Dairy Products

Curriculum Areas

Science   Math
Language Arts

Preparation Tools and Materials

- One sheet of yellow tagboard
- One sheet of light blue tagboard
- Construction paper or sentence strips
- Markers
- Glue or glue stick
- Scissors (craft scissors optional)
- Lamination paper

Directions

1. On the sheet of yellow tagboard using scissors and markers, draw a large cheese wedge and cut it out (see the accompanying photo).

2. Using construction paper and markers, illustrate the macaroni and cheese ingredients, including macaroni noodles, butter, salt, pepper, flour, milk, and cheese cubes.

3. On construction paper or sentence strips, type or use a marker to print the following ingredients for macaroni and cheese:

   WHAT YOU NEED:
   3–3½ cups cooked macaroni
   ¼ cup butter
   ½ teaspoon salt
   ½ teaspoon pepper
   ¼ cup flour
   1½ cups milk
   ½ pound cubed cheese

4. Using glue, attach the word strips and illustrations to the cheese wedge shape, using the accompanying figure as a guide.

5. On construction paper or sentence strips, type or use a marker to print the following recipe for macaroni and cheese.

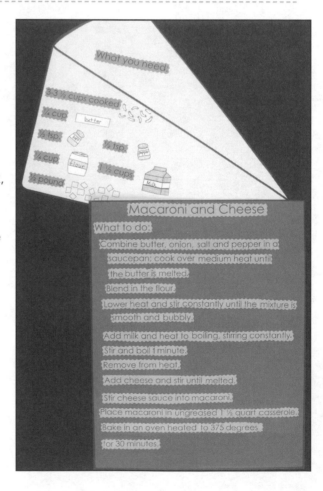

Science

142   (continues)

Recipe Chart: Macaroni and Cheese

(continued)

MACARONI AND CHEESE
WHAT TO DO:

Combine butter, salt, and pepper in a saucepan and cook over medium heat until the butter is melted.

Blend in the flour.

Lower heat and stir constantly until the mixture is smooth and bubbly.

Add milk and heat to boiling, stirring constantly.

Stir and boil 1 minute.

Remove from heat.

Add cheese and stir until melted.

Stir cheese sauce into macaroni.

Place macaroni in ungreased 1½ quart casserole.

Bake in an oven heated to 375 degrees for 30 minutes.

6. Using glue, attach the recipe steps in order on the blue tagboard.

7. Laminate both charts.

Teaching/Learning Strategies

- Gather the supplies and ingredients for making macaroni and cheese for lunch or a snack. Refer to the charts while making the recipe. Have the children help as much as safely possible.

Science

Recipe Chart: Pudding

Developmental Goals

1. Develop an appreciation for the printed word.
2. Practice following directions.
3. Observe changes in substances.
4. Practice measuring ingredients.
5. Associate spoken words with written words.
6. Develop left-to-right progression skills.

Related Curriculum Themes
Cooking
Foods

Curriculum Areas
Science   Language Arts
Math

Preparation Tools and Materials

- One sheet of tagboard (light brown)
- Construction paper or sentence strips
- Markers
- Scissors (craft scissors optional)
- Glue or glue stick
- Package of pudding mix
- Lamination paper

Directions

1. On the construction paper or a sentence strip, type or use a marker to print the title "Pudding."

2. Using glue, attach the title strip to the top of the tagboard (see the accompanying photo).

3. Cut off the front label of the package of pudding mix.

4. Using construction paper, markers, and scissors, make a bowl shape, a milk carton shape, and a wire whisk shape.

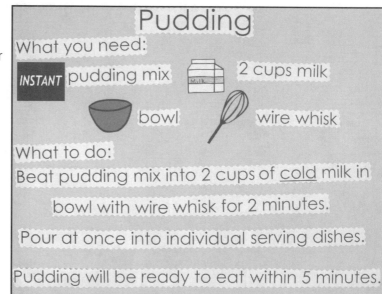

Pudding

What you need:

INSTANT pudding mix   2 cups milk

bowl   wire whisk

What to do:

Beat pudding mix into 2 cups of <u>cold</u> milk in bowl with wire whisk for 2 minutes.

Pour at once into individual serving dishes.

Pudding will be ready to eat within 5 minutes.

Science

5. On construction paper or sentence strips, type or use a marker to print the following pudding ingredients and recipe steps:

PUDDING
WHAT YOU NEED:
Pudding mix
Bowl
2 cups of milk
Wire whisk

Recipe Chart: Pudding

(continued)

WHAT TO DO:
Beat pudding mix into 2 cups of cold milk in a bowl with wire whisk for 2 minutes. Pour at once into individual serving dishes. Pudding will be ready to eat within 5 minutes.

6. Using glue, attach the word strips, ingredient shapes, and tool shapes to the chart.

7. Laminate the chart.

Teaching/Learning Strategies

- Use the chart with the children to make pudding for a snack. Be sure the children wash their hands before participating in any cooking project. Afterward, display the chart in the classroom for the children to recall the procedures and the pudding ingredients.

Science

145

Sensory Shakers

Developmental Goals

1. Develop visual discrimination skills.
2. Observe changes and movement.
3. Develop small muscle coordination skills.

Related Curriculum Themes

Senses   Containers
Colors   Movement
Shapes

Curriculum Area

Science

Preparation Tools and Materials

- Clear plastic bottles with lids
- Mineral oil
- Glitter
- Small beads
- Sequins
- Food coloring

Directions

1. Fill the clear plastic bottles with mineral oil.

2. Add different items to each bottle. For example, put beads in one bottle. Put glitter in a second bottle. Place sequins in a third bottle. Add a few drops of food coloring to a bottle, if desired.

3. Secure a lid on each bottle.

Teaching/Learning Strategies

- Place the sensory shakers on a table in the science area of the classroom. Encourage the children to shake or turn each bottle and to observe the movement of the items.

- When there are enough materials, have the children help make their own sensory shakers.

Science

Sequencing Cards

Developmental Goals

1. Practice sequencing skills.
2. Develop visual discrimination skills.
3. Develop problem-solving skills.
4. Develop eye-hand coordination skills.

Related Curriculum Theme
My World

Curriculum Areas
Language Arts   Math

Preparation Tools and Materials

- One sheet of white tagboard
- Markers
- Scissors
- Lamination paper

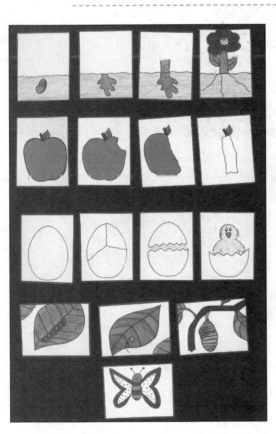

Directions

1. Cut the tagboard into identically sized pieces.
2. Using four tagboard pieces, draw a four-step picture (see the accompanying photo). Examples include the growth of a flower seed, eating an apple, a chick hatching from an egg, and the life cycle of a butterfly.
3. Laminate all pieces.

Teaching/Learning Strategies

- Show the children a four-step picture in a mixed-up order. Have them tell you which card comes first, which card comes second, which card comes third, and which card comes fourth or last. Then, ask the children to describe each step. Also consider using the cards for independent work. The children can sort the sets of cards and sequence them.

Science

Shades of Colors Chart

Developmental Goals

1. Identify colors.
2. Practice sequencing colors from lightest to darkest.
3. Develop visual discrimination skills.
4. Practice sorting.
5. Develop eye-hand coordination skills.

Related Curriculum Themes

Colors   Sense of Sight
Art

Curriculum Areas

Science
Art

Preparation Tools and Materials

- One sheet of white tagboard
- Construction paper or sentence strips
- Markers
- Ruler or straight edge
- Scissors
- Paint chip sample cards of various colors
- Glue or glue stick
- Lamination paper

Directions

1. On the construction paper or a sentence strip, type or use a marker to print the caption "Lightest to Darkest."

2. Using glue, attach the caption to the top portion of the tagboard (see the accompanying photo).

3. Using a marker and a straight edge, create a grid of approximately 32 squares.

4. Type or use a marker to print the word "Lightest" in the top row of the grid.

5. Type or use a marker to print the word "Darkest" in the bottom row of the grid.

6. Cut the paint chip cards apart.

7. Laminate the chart and paint color cards.

Science

Teaching/Learning Strategies

- After introducing the chart and paint chips to the children, place the items on a table or the floor. Encourage the children to first sort the paint chip cards by color families, then to place the paint chip cards on the chart in order from lightest to darkest.

Sink or Float Chart

Developmental Goals

1. Learn sinking and floating concepts.
2. Develop classification skills.
3. Develop observation and prediction skills.
4. Explore water properties.
5. Develop curiosity.
6. Practice the prosocial behavior of taking turns.

Related Curriculum Themes

Water   Sinking/Floating
Science

Curriculum Areas

Science
Language Arts

Preparation Tools and Materials

- One sheet of light blue tagboard, 10" x 14"
- Sixteen library book pockets
- Sixteen white note cards, 3" x 5"
- Black felt-tip marker
- Ruler
- Rubber cement or glue
- Craft knife
- Lamination paper

Directions

1. Across the top of the tagboard, print the title "Do the items sink or float?" (see the accompanying photo).
2. Using a ruler and a marker, underline the title and divide the tagboard in half.
3. Print the word "Sink" on the left side of the tagboard and "Float" on the right side.
4. Next to the words "Sink" and "Float," draw simple pictures of sinking and floating.
5. Glue eight library pockets to the left side of the tagboard and eight to the right side as shown in the accompanying photo.
6. On eight notecards, print the names of different objects that sink. Items could include crayon, rubber band, pencil, metal spoon, feather, button, shell, nail, ping-pong ball, sponge, corn, rock, plastic spoon, scissors, block, clothespins, paintbrush, and marble. Consider using the items in the preceding step.

Science

7. On the eight remaining notecards, print the names of different objects that float.
8. Next to the names on the notecards, draw the objects simply.
9. Laminate the chart and pieces.
10. Using a craft knife, carefully slit the library pockets open.

Teaching/Learning Strategies

- Collect the items on the cards and a small tub of water. One at a time, have the children place items in the tub. Then, ask the children if the items sink or float. After this, ask the children to take the cards with the items and place the cards in pockets on the appropriate sides of the chart.

Smelly Socks

Developmental Goals

1. Develop an awareness of the sense of smell.
2. Develop visual discrimination skills.
3. Practice problem solving skills.
4. Practice the prosocial behavior of taking turns.

Related Curriculum Themes

Senses   Socks
Feel

Curriculum Area

Science

Preparation Tools and Materials

- Safe items with identifiable smells (e.g., coffee grounds, cocoa powder, peanut butter, honey, spices)
- Assortment of clean socks

Directions

1. Place a small amount of an aromatic substance in the toe area of each sock.

Teaching/Learning Strategies

- Introduce the smelly socks to the children during a large group activity. Pass one sock around the circle, and encourage the children to identify the smell. Continue until all socks have been passed around and their smells identified. Afterward, place the smelly socks on a table in the classroom for the children to use independently.

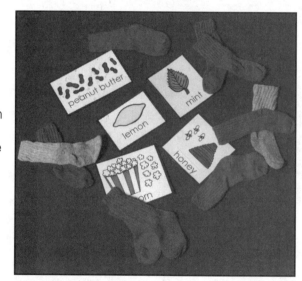

Science

Soda Bottle Terrarium

Developmental Goals

1. Observe the growth cycle of a plant.
2. Identify plant needs.
3. Name plant parts.
4. Learn how to reuse materials.

Related Curriculum Themes

Plants   Containers
Water   Bottles
Gardens

Curriculum Area

Science

Preparation Tools and Materials

- One liter soda bottle (empty and clean)
- Craft knife or scissors
- Potting soil
- Small plant or seeds
- Water

Directions

1. Remove the label from the soda bottle.
2. Using a craft knife, cut all the way around the bottle, approximately 4 inches from the bottom.
3. Fill the soda bottle bottom with potting soil.
4. Insert a small plant in the soil, or press a few seeds into the soil.
5. Gently water the plant.
6. Place the top section of the soda bottle over the bottom portion.

Teaching/Learning Strategies

- Place the plant in the science area of the classroom, or use it to decorate the room. Make one child responsible for watering the plant as needed. If desired, prepare a chart and place it by the plant, recording how often the plant is watered.

Science

Texture Cards

Developmental Goals

1. Develop tactile discrimination skills.
2. Differentiate between rough and smooth.
3. Develop expressive language skills.
4. Develop problem-solving skills.

Related Curriculum Themes

My Five Senses   Texture
Fabric

Curriculum Area

Science

Preparation Tools and Materials

- Fabric remnants (various textures)
- Sandpaper scrap
- Glue or glue gun
- Tagboard pieces, 4" x 4"

Directions

1. Using a wide variety of textures, glue fabric pieces and sandpaper to the tagboard pieces.
2. Trim the edges of the tagboard.

Teaching/Learning Strategies

- Present the texture cards as an individual or a small group activity. Encourage the children to feel and describe each texture card.

- When developmentally appropriate and to provide a challenge, have the children sequence the cards from smoothest to roughest.

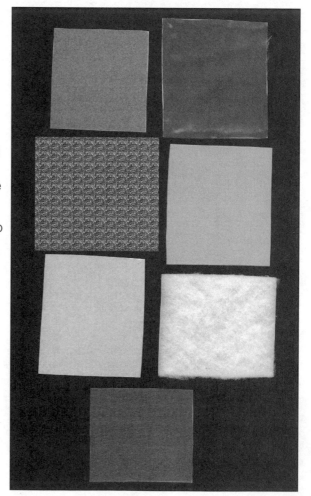

Toothpaste

Developmental Goals

1. Practice predicting.
2. Develop new vocabulary words.
3. Develop observation skills.
4. Learn measuring skills.
5. Practice following directions.
6. Practice left-to-right progression skills.
7. Observe changes in a substance.
8. Develop an appreciation for the printed word.
9. Understand printed words and meanings.
10. Develop a desire to read.

Related Curriculum Themes

Health   Brushes
Dentist   My Body
Teeth

Curriculum Areas

Science   Social Studies
Math

Preparation Tools and Materials

- One piece of tagboard, 22" x 28"
- Watercolor markers
- Label from a salt container
- Front panel of a baking soda box
- Glue or glue stick
- Lamination paper

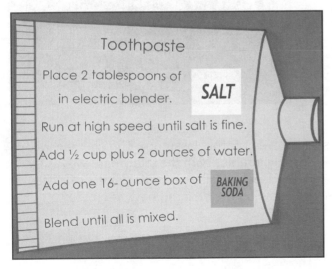

Toothpaste

Place 2 tablespoons of **SALT** in electric blender.

Run at high speed until salt is fine.

Add ½ cup plus 2 ounces of water.

Add one 16-ounce box of **BAKING SODA**

Blend until all is mixed.

Directions

1. Cut the tagboard in the shape of a tube of toothpaste (see the accompanying photo).

2. Using a marker, add details to the shape as desired.

3. Type or use a marker to print the following title and directions on the tagboard shape:

   TOOTHPASTE
   Place 2 tablespoons of salt in an electric blender.
   Run at high speed until the salt is fine.
   Add ½ cup plus 2 ounces of water.
   Add a 16 ounce box of baking soda.
   Blend until all is mixed.

4. Add illustrations, if desired.

5. Laminate the chart.

Science

Teaching/Learning Strategies

- Collect the tools for making toothpaste, including serving spoons, an electric blender, measuring cups, and a container to hold the toothpaste. Then, collect the ingredients, including 2 tablespoons of salt, a box of baking soda, and ½ cup plus 2 ounces of water. If desired, add peppermint flavoring and food coloring.

- Encourage the children to observe the blending of ingredients. After lunch, give the children toothpaste with which to brush their teeth.

Wave Jar

Related Curriculum Themes

Water   Movement
Ocean

Curriculum Area

Science

Preparation Tools and Materials

- One clear plastic container
- Mineral oil
- Blue food coloring
- Water
- Rubber cement

Directions

1. Fill the plastic container halfway with water and add several drops of blue food coloring.
2. Fill the remainder of the container with mineral oil.
3. Pour rubber cement into the cap of the container.
4. Screw on the cap, wiping off excess rubber cement.
5. Allow the container to dry before use.

Teaching/Learning Strategies

- Prepare and place the wave jar in the science area of the classroom. The children will learn about their physical world as they playfully interact with the jar. Create waves by slowly tilting the container. If needed, you, the teacher, may serve as guide or facilitator, demonstrating an interest in the jar and showing the children how to create waves.

- When developmentally appropriate, have the children prepare their own wave jars.

Science

Weather Chart

Developmental Goals

1. Develop an appreciation for the printed word.
2. Identify types of weather.
3. Associate symbols with weather types.
4. Develop visual discrimination skills.
5. Recognize that spoken words can be represented in print.

Related Curriculum Themes
Weather
School

Curriculum Areas
Science
Language Arts

Preparation Tools and Materials

- One sheet of tagboard (light blue)
- Construction paper or sentence strips
- Markers
- Scissors
- Glue or glue stick
- Light blue transparency
- Brass fastener
- Lamination paper

Directions

1. On the construction paper or sentence strips, type or use a marker to print the caption "The weather today is . . ." and such related weather words as *sunny, rainy, hot, windy, partly cloudy, cloudy, cold,* and *snowy.*

2. Using glue, attach the caption and weather words to the tagboard (see the accompanying photo).

3. Above each weather word, use markers to draw a picture that represents the word. For example, draw a sun above the word "sunny," draw a snowflake above the word "snowy."

4. Laminate the chart.

5. From the light blue transparency, cut two arrows.

6. Using a brass fastener, attach the two arrows to the center of the tagboard.

Teaching/Learning Strategies

- Use the weather chart during classroom opening activities. Move the arrows on the chart to show the day's weather. Display the chart on a bulletin board or wall.

Science

What's Wrong with the Pictures?

Developmental Goals

1. Develop visual discrimination skills.
2. Develop expressive language skills.
3. Develop eye-hand coordination skills.
4. Develop problem-solving skills.

Related Curriculum Themes
Communication
Adaptable to Any Theme

Curriculum Areas
Science
Language Arts

Preparation Tools and Materials

- One sheet of tagboard, 16" x 20"
- Watercolor markers
- Crayon, grease pencil, or watercolor marker
- Glue or glue stick
- Felt scraps
- Scissors
- Lamination paper

Directions

1. Cut the tagboard into 16 cards, 4" x 5".

2. On each card, draw a simple picture with an obvious error (see the accompanying photo).

3. Laminate each card.

Teaching/Learning Strategies

- In a small group or when interacting with a child, present the pictures. Ask the child what is wrong with each card. If the child hesitates, provide clues.

Science

Worm Farm

Developmental Goals

1. Develop an appreciation for nature.
2. Develop visual discrimination and observation skills.
3. Learn science concepts through meaningful experiences.
4. Experience a print-rich environment.

Related Curriculum Themes

Soil	Plants
Gardens	Animals

Curriculum Areas

Science
Language Arts

Preparation Tools and Materials

- One sheet of tagboard
- Construction paper
- Watercolor markers
- Scissors
- Glue or glue stick
- Lamination paper

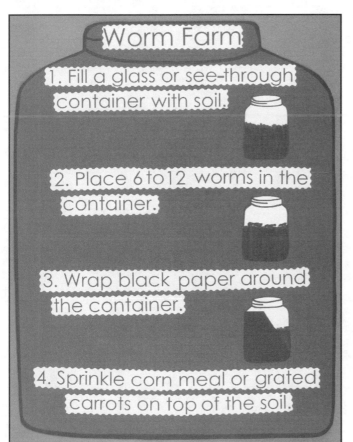

Directions

1. Cut the tagboard sheet to resemble a large jar (see the accompanying photo).

2. On the construction paper, type or use a marker to print the following directions and draw corresponding illustrations:

   WORM FARM
   a. Fill a glass or see-through container with soil.
   b. Place 6 to 12 worms in the container.
   c. Wrap black paper around the container.
   d. Sprinkle corn meal or grated carrot on top of the soil.

3. Using glue, attach the directions and illustrations to the tagboard shape.

4. Laminate the chart.

Teaching/Learning Strategies

- Gather the materials for the worm farm and allow the children to help prepare it. Tell the children that the black paper around the jar helps keep light out of the jar, encouraging the worms to locate near the outside of the container. Periodically, remove the black paper briefly and allow the children to observe the worms and their trails. After the children have lost interest in the farm, let them free the worms outdoors in a garden or flower garden.

Science

157

Social Studies

Good
Deed
Box

Birthday Chart

Developmental Goals

1. Develop an appreciation for the printed word.
2. Develop self-esteem.
3. Become familiar with the names of months.
4. Observe one's name in print.

Related Curriculum Themes

Birthdays   Family
Friends   Celebrations

Curriculum Areas

Social Studies   Math
Language Arts

Preparation Tools and Materials

- One sheet of tagboard
- Birthday wrapping paper
- Markers
- Scissors
- Glue or tape
- Construction paper or sentence strips
- Ruler or straight edge
- Lamination paper

Directions

1. On the construction paper or sentence strips, type or use a marker to print the question, "What month were you born?"

2. Using glue, attach the question to the top of the tagboard (see the accompanying photo).

3. On construction paper or sentence strips, type or use a marker to print the names of the months.

4. Using glue, attach along the left side of the tagboard the months in order.

5. Using a marker and a straight edge, create a row and column for each month.

6. Using birthday wrapping paper, create a border or frame for the tagboard sheet.

7. Laminate the chart.

What month were you born?	
January	
February	
March	
April	
May	
June	
July	
August	
September	
October	
November	
December	

Teaching/Learning Strategies

- Introduce the birthday chart to the children during a group time activity. If the children can print their names, they can take turns writing their names in the columns of their birthday months. After all children's names are on the chart, have the children help you count the children who have birthdays in the month of January. Continue for all months. Which months have the most birthdays in your class? Display the completed chart in the classroom.

Social Studies

Birthday Crowns

Developmental Goals

1. Develop self-esteem.
2. Recognize letters.
3. Identify names.
4. Experience a print-rich environment.
5. Develop visual discrimination skills.

Related Curriculum Themes
Celebrations
Birthdays

Curriculum Area
Social Studies

Preparation Tools and Materials
- Construction paper in assorted colors
- Colored markers
- Scissors
- Glitter
- Glue or glue stick
- Lamination paper

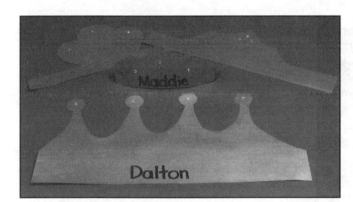

Directions

1. On construction paper, trace a crown pattern and cut it out (see the accompanying photo).
2. Using glitter and markers, decorate the crown.
3. Print the child's name and age on the crown.
4. Laminate the crown.

Teaching/Learning Strategies

- If desired, have the birthday child choose the color of the crown. Older children may enjoy decorating their own crowns, as well as printing their names on them. Allow the children to wear their crowns on their birthdays. During snack, lunch, or group time, sing "Happy Birthday" to the birthday child.

- *Note:* Not all families celebrate birthdays. Please be aware of families' beliefs and wishes.

Social Studies

Favorite Color Chart

Developmental Goals

1. Associate the printed word with the spoken word.
2. Record data.
3. Develop classification skills.
4. Review color concepts.
5. Observe one's name in print.
6. Develop visual discrimination skills.

Related Curriculum Themes

Art   Communication
Colors   I'm Me, I'm Special

Curriculum Areas

Social Studies   Math
Language Arts

Preparation Tools and Materials

- One sheet of white tagboard
- Construction paper in various colors
- Black marker
- Ruler or yardstick
- Scissors
- Lamination paper

Directions

1. Across the top of the tagboard, print the question "Which color do you like the best?" (see the accompanying photo).

2. Draw a horizontal line under the title.

3. Divide the remaining tagboard into six equal sections.

4. Label each section with a color word.

5. Decorate the chart as desired.

Which color do you like the best?

red	Drew	
orange	Logan	
yellow	Christian Lizzie	
green		
blue	Lucas	
purple		

6. From various colors of construction paper, prepare crayon shapes, approximately 5" long.

7. Laminate the chart.

Teaching/Learning Strategies

- Introduce the chart to the children in a group setting. Have the children place their names under their favorite colors.

- When developmentally appropriate, have the children print their names in the color crayon of their choice. The children can also print their names on the chart using watercolor markers. Vary the color choices.

Feelings Chart

Related Curriculum Themes

Feelings   Friends
School

Curriculum Areas

Social Studies   Math
Health

Preparation Tools and Materials

- One sheet of white tagboard
- Construction paper or sentence strips
- Markers
- Scissors
- Glue or glue stick
- Stickers or clip art (optional)
- Ruler or straight edge
- Lamination paper

Directions

1. Across the top of the tagboard, use a marker to print the question "How are you feeling today?" (see the accompanying photo).

2. From construction paper, cut four 5" circles.

3. On each circle, use a marker to draw a face that depicts a feeling: happy, sad, tired, and angry.

4. Using glue, attach the face circles horizontally on the tagboard under the caption.

5. Using a marker and a straight edge, create a column for each feeling.

6. Decorate the chart with stickers or clip art, if desired.

7. Laminate the chart.

Teaching/Learning Strategies

- Introduce the chart to the children in a large group setting. Encourage the children to express how they are feeling that day. The children or you, the teacher, can use a watercolor marker to print the children's names in the corresponding column. When the chart is complete, count the people who feel happy, sad, and so on.

Social Studies

Good Deed Box

Related Curriculum Themes

Friends   Feelings
School

Curriculum Area

Social Studies

Preparation Tools and Materials

- One box with a lid (any size or shape)
- Construction paper
- Scissors
- Markers
- Glue or glue stick
- Stickers or clip art
- Marbles

Directions

1. On a piece of construction paper, type or use a marker to print the title "Good Deed Box."

2. Using glue, attach the title to the box lid (see the accompanying photo).

3. Decorate the lid and sides of the box with stickers or clip art.

Teaching/Learning Strategies

- Introduce the "Good Deed Box" to the children in a large group setting. Talk about which behaviors and acts are "good deeds." Place the box and some marbles in a special area of the classroom. Decide what will be done when the box is full of marbles. Perhaps a special activity or treat will be the reward for filling the box with "good deeds."

Social
Studies

Good Deed Bucket

Developmental Goals

1. Develop self-esteem.
2. Participate in a group activity.
3. Identify acts of kindness.
4. Develop an appreciation for the printed word.
5. Develop prosocial behaviors.

Related Curriculum Themes
Friends   Feelings
School

Curriculum Area
Social Studies

Preparation Tools and Materials
- One metal or plastic bucket
- Construction paper
- Scissors
- Markers
- Glue or glue stick
- Clothespins (optional)
- Marbles

Directions

1. On a strip of construction paper, type or use a marker to print the title "Good Deed Bucket."

2. Using glue, attach the strip to the outside of the bucket (see the accompanying photo).

3. On another strip of construction paper, type or print the following verse:

   Do a good deed and a marble will go in.
   When the bucket is full, a reward we all will win!

4. Using clothespins, attach the strip to the handles of the bucket.

Teaching/Learning Strategies

- Introduce the "Good Deed Bucket" to the children in a large group setting. Talk about which behaviors and acts are "good deeds." Place the bucket and some marbles in a special area of the classroom, like the teacher's desk, a window sill, or a small table. Let the children decide what the special reward will be when the bucket is full of marbles.

"How Did You Get to School Today?" Chart

Developmental Goals

1. Develop classification skills.
2. Observe printed words.
3. Identify modes of transportation.
4. Associate spoken words with printed words.

Related Curriculum Themes

Transportation   School
Wheels   Families

Curriculum Areas

Social Studies   Language Arts
Science   Math

Preparation Tools and Materials

- One sheet of light colored tagboard
- Markers
- Ruler
- Scissors
- Construction paper
- Glue or glue stick
- Transportation stickers or clip art
- Index cards
- Lamination paper

Directions

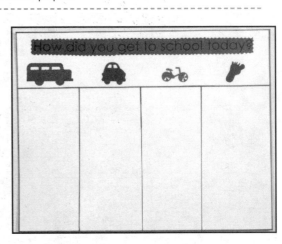

1. Across the top of the light colored tagboard, type or use a marker to print the caption "How did you get to school today?" (see the accompanying photo).

2. Using a ruler and a marker, divide the remaining tagboard sheet vertically into four equal sections.

3. On construction paper, draw a school bus, a car, and a bicycle and cut out the shapes.

4. Glue each shape to the top of one of the four columns.

5. In the remaining column, type or use a marker to print the word "Other."

6. Decorate the edges of the chart with transportation stickers or clip art pictures as desired.

7. Laminate the chart.

8. Print the names of the children on index cards or construction paper using a marker.

Teaching/Learning Strategies

- Introduce the chart during large group time. Encourage the children to place their name cards under the transportation they used to get to school.

- When developmentally appropriate, have the children print their own name cards.

"I Can" Chart

Developmental Goals

1. Develop self-esteem.
2. Practice physical activities or skills.
3. Develop an appreciation for the printed word.
4. Develop visual discrimination skills.
5. Develop a sense of group belonging.

Related Curriculum Themes

Creative Movement
My Body

Curriculum Areas

Social Studies   Language Arts
Physical Education

Preparation Tools and Materials

- One sheet of tagboard
- Construction paper or sentence strips
- Markers
- Glue or glue stick
- Scissors
- Stickers
- Ruler or straight edge
- Lamination paper

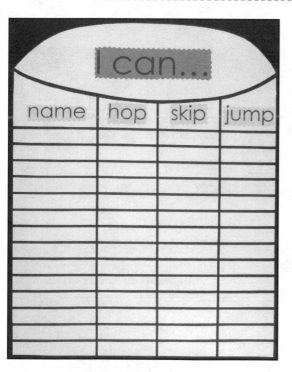

Directions

1. Using scissors, round the top corners of the tagboard (see the accompanying photo).

2. On construction paper or sentence strips, type or use a marker to print the following captions:

   I can . . .
   Name
   Hop
   Skip
   Jump

3. Using glue, attach the words to the tagboard, using the accompanying photo as a guide. Glue the words "I can . . ." to the top of the tagboard. Glue the words "Name," "Hop," "Skip," and "Jump" in a row under the main caption.

4. Using a ruler and marker, create columns for each word.

5. Using a ruler and marker, make horizontal lines to create a grid.

6. Decorate the top of the tagboard with stickers.

7. Laminate the chart.

Teaching/Learning Strategies

- Use a watercolor marker to print each child's name below the name column. Display the chart in the classroom. As children master the physical skills of hopping, skipping, and jumping, record the accomplishments on the chart. Praise all efforts.

Social Studies

Make a Halloween Card

Developmental Goals

1. Develop an appreciation for the printed word.
2. Develop visual discrimination skills.
3. Develop problem-solving skills.
4. Develop eye-hand coordination skills.
5. Practice forming alphabet letters.
6. Develop small muscle coordination skills.

Related Curriculum Themes

Halloween	The Alphabet
Communication	Our Friends
Holidays	Writing

Curriculum Areas

Social Studies Language Arts

Preparation Tools and Materials

- One sheet of black tagboard
- Orange and green construction paper
- Manuscript paper or sentence strips
- Markers
- Scissors (craft scissors optional)
- Glue or glue stick
- Lamination paper

Directions

1. Cut six strips of manuscript paper or sentence strips (see the accompanying photo).

2. Print each of the following lines on the manuscript paper or sentence strips:

   MAKE A HALLOWEEN CARD.
   Have a happy Halloween.
   Trick or treat!
   Carve a pumpkin.
   I like your silly costume.

3. Glue each manuscript strip to pieces of orange construction paper that are large enough to leave a ¼" border.

4. From orange construction paper, cut two pumpkins, and add a green stem to each.

5. Glue the pumpkins to the chart.

6. Laminate the chart.

Teaching/Learning Strategies

- Place the chart in the writing center or language arts area of the classroom. Give the children colored pencils, markers, and paper to make Halloween cards. If available, also provide clip art and Halloween stickers for the children to decorate the cards.

Social Studies

Make a Valentine

Developmental Goals

1. Make a Valentine by selecting and copying a greeting.
2. Develop an appreciation for the printed word.
3. Develop visual discrimination skills.
4. Develop problem-solving skills.
5. Develop eye-hand coordination skills.
6. Practice forming alphabet letters.
7. Develop small muscle coordination skills.

Related Curriculum Themes

Holidays   Communication
Writing   Friends
Valentine's Day   Symbols

Curriculum Areas

Social Studies
Language Arts

Preparation Tools and Materials

- One sheet of red or pink tagboard
- Manuscript or writing paper
- Markers
- Scissors (craft scissors optional)
- Glue or glue stick
- Lamination paper

Directions

1. On a manuscript strip, print the title "Make a Valentine." (See the accompanying photo.)

2. On strips of manuscript paper, print such Valentine messages as the following:

   Happy Valentine's Day!
   Be my Valentine.
   You are as sweet as candy.
   I want you for my Valentine.
   I love you.
   Have a heart, Valentine.

3. Glue the strips to the tagboard.

4. Using a black, broad-tipped marker, draw a frame around the tagboard.

5. If desired, draw hearts or add some heart stickers.

6. Laminate the chart.

Teaching/Learning Strategies

- Place the chart in the writing center or language arts area of the classroom. Give the children colored pencils, markers, and paper to make Valentines. If available, also provide Valentine stickers and clip art for the children to decorate the cards.

Social Studies

My Family Frame

Developmental Goals

1. Represent family members visually.
2. Print the names of family members.
3. Record a number representing the members of one's family.
4. Practice communicating in writing.
5. Develop eye-hand coordination skills.
6. Develop a sense of group belonging.

Related Curriculum Themes

Families
Numerals
Alphabet Letters
Communication
Names

Drawing
Brothers and Sisters
Writing Tools
Art

Curriculum Areas

Social Studies   Language Arts

Preparation Tools and Materials

- One large sheet of tagboard
- Markers

- Scissors (craft scissors optional)
- Lamination paper

Directions

1. Draw a horizontal line across the midline of the tagboard.

2. Cut the tagboard in half.

3. Turn the tagboard vertical.

4. Print the title "My Family" at the top of the tagboard (see the accompanying photo).

5. Draw a picture frame on the tagboard.

6. Using a brown felt-tip marker, color in the frame.

7. If desired, add detail by outlining the frame and adding corner angles and distress marks.

8. Print the following under each frame:

   I have _____ people in my family.
   Their names are _____.

9. Laminate the chart.

Teaching/Learning Strategies

- Place this chart in the writing or language arts center for children with manuscript skills. Provide paper, colored pencils, and markers. If needed, give the children a model for each family member's name.

Pond Attendance Chart

Developmental Goals

1. Develop a sense of group belonging.
2. Develop self-esteem.
3. Identify one's name in print.
4. Develop an appreciation for the printed word.
5. Develop visual discrimination skills.

Related Curriculum Themes
Frogs   School
Friends

Curriculum Areas
Social Studies
Language Arts

Preparation Tools and Materials
- One sheet of light blue tagboard
- Construction paper or sentence strips
- Frog-shaped note paper
- Frog stickers or clip art
- Markers
- Scissors (craft scissors optional)
- Glue or glue stick
- Tape
- Lamination paper

Directions

1. On construction paper or a sentence strip, type or use a marker to print the question "Who came to the pond today?"

2. Using glue, attach the caption to the top of the tagboard (see the accompanying photo).

3. Using stickers or clip art, decorate the tagboard.

4. On a sheet of frog-shaped note paper, print each student's name.

5. Laminate the chart and frog pieces.

Teaching/Learning Strategies

- Place the chart, frogs, and tape near the classroom entrance. Explain to the children that when they arrive at school, they should use tape to hang the frogs with their names. Children will soon embrace this routine, and the activity will help you, the teacher, take attendance.

Social Studies

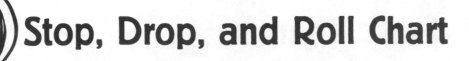

Stop, Drop, and Roll Chart

Developmental Goals

1. Develop an appreciation for the printed word.
2. Practice fire safety procedures.
3. Practice following directions.
4. Develop visual discrimination skills.
5. Recognize that spoken words can be represented in print.

Related Curriculum Themes

Firefighters   Home
Safety   School

Curriculum Areas

Social Studies   Language Arts
Health

Preparation Tools and Materials

- One sheet of red tagboard
- Construction paper or sentence strips
- Markers
- Glue or glue stick
- Scissors (craft scissors optional)
- Ruler or straight edge
- Lamination paper

Directions

1. On construction paper or sentence strips, type or use a marker to print the following (see the accompanying photo):

   Clothes on fire?
   What do you do?
   Stop, drop, and roll on the ground,
   If you want to keep a fire from spreading around!

2. Using glue, attach the fire safety directions to the tagboard.

3. Using construction paper, markers, and scissors, draw a person in the "stop," "drop," and "roll" position and cut out the drawings.

4. Using glue, attach the illustrations close to the bottom of the tagboard.

5. Using a marker and straight edge, create a rectangle under each illustration.

6. On construction paper rectangles, type or print the words "Stop," "Drop," and "Roll."

7. Decorate the chart with safety scissors or clip art, if desired.

8. Laminate the chart and word cards.

Teaching/Learning Strategies

- Use the chart in your classroom when talking about fire safety. Display the chart in the classroom, and allow the children to tape the word cards under the corresponding pictures.

Social Studies

172